The Owner of This Book

_____

Was Created to Be Fruitful

Copyright © 2016 by Sharon Arpana Edwards.
All rights reserved.

Published in the United States by Consonant Books
P.O. Box 236, Pasadena, CA 91102
sharonarpana.com

No part of this publication may be reproduced, stored in a retrieval system, or transmitted in any form or by any means—electronic, mechanical, photocopying, audio or video recording, or other—without the prior written permission of the publisher.

Unless otherwise noted, all Scripture quotations are taken from the New King James Version®. Copyright © 1982 by Thomas Nelson. Used by permission. All rights reserved.

Scripture quotations marked (ESV) are from the ESV® Bible (The Holy Bible, English Standard Version®), copyright © 2001 by Crossway, a publishing ministry of Good News Publishers. Used by permission. All rights reserved.

Scripture quotations marked (KJV) are from the Holy Bible, the King James Version. Public domain.

Scripture quotations marked (NASB) are taken from the New American Standard Bible® (NASB), Copyright © 1960, 1962, 1963, 1968, 1971, 1972, 1973, 1975, 1977, 1995 by The Lockman Foundation. Used by permission. www.Lockman.org

Scripture quotations marked (NIV) are taken from the Holy Bible, New International Version®, NIV®. Copyright © 1973, 1978, 1984, 2011 by Biblica, Inc.™ Used by permission of Zondervan. All rights reserved worldwide. www.Zondervan.com

All italics in Scripture quotations have been added by the author.

Library of Congress Control Number: 2016917802
ISBN: 978-0-9893233-3-8

BISAC Subject Headings:
RELIGION / Christian Living / Devotional
RELIGION / Biblical Studies / Old Testament / Pentateuch
RELIGION / Biblical Meditations / General

Printed in the United States of America
FIRST EDITION

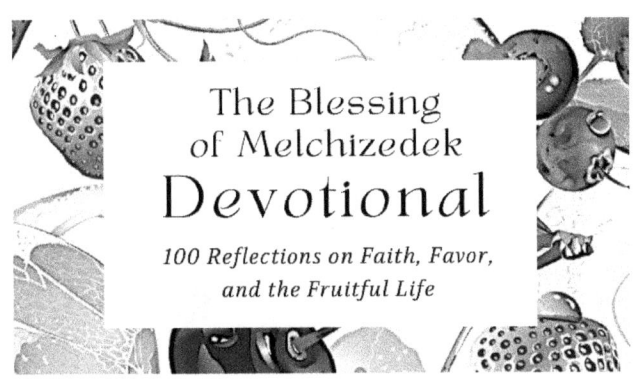

The Blessing of Melchizedek
Devotional

100 Reflections on Faith, Favor, and the Fruitful Life

Sharon Arpana Edwards

CONSONANT BOOKS

For my mother,
Lalita Edwards,
who taught me to have
my daily devotions,
mostly by example.

Her children rise up and call her blessed.
Proverbs 31:28

Jesus says:

I am the vine, you are the branches. He who abides in Me, and I in him, bears much fruit; for without Me you can do nothing.

If you abide in Me, and My words abide in you, you will ask what you desire, and it shall be done for you.

By this My Father is glorified, that you bear much fruit; so you will be My disciples.

As the Father loved Me, I also have loved you; abide in My love.

If you keep My commandments, you will abide in My love, just as I have kept My Father's commandments and abide in His love.

These things I have spoken to you, that My joy may remain in you, and that your joy may be full.

You did not choose Me, but I chose you and appointed you that you should go and bear fruit, and that your fruit should remain, that whatever you ask the Father in My name He may give you.

—JOHN 15:5,7-11,16

Contents

Introduction	1
PROLOGUE	9
A Promise of Blessing: *Days 1–3*	11
PART ONE: THE CONTEXT	17
The Valley of Shaveh: *Days 4–9*	19
The Vale of Siddim: *Days 10–13*	31
The Context of Promise: *Days 14–18*	39
PART TWO: THE KING	49
Melchizedek: *Days 19–23*	51
King of Righteousness: *Days 24–28*	61
The Rule of Righteousness: *Days 29–36*	71
King of Salem: *Days 37–39*	87
The Prince of Peace: *Days 40–45*	93
PART THREE: THE PRIEST	105
Priest of God Most High: *Days 46–48*	107
The Aaronic Order: *Days 49–51*	113
The Order of Melchizedek: Days 52–56	119
Melchizedek's Table: Days 57–61	129

PART FOUR: THE BLESSED	139
Abram of God: *Days 62–66*	141
Abram and Abraham: *Days 67–70*	151
The Faith of Abraham: *Days 71–77*	159
Abram's Altars: *Days 78–82*	173
Blessed Be God: *Days 83–86*	183
PART FIVE: THE RESPONSE	191
Abram to Melchizedek: *Days 87–90*	193
Abram to Bera: *Days 91–93*	201
God to Abram: *Days 94–97*	207
EPILOGUE	215
The Promised Son: *Days 98–100*	217

Introduction

The question I have been asked most often about *The Blessing of Melchizedek*, the book that got converted into this devotional, concerns the identity of my title character. Not surprisingly, people want to know if I think he was a preincarnate appearance of Jesus. I have discussed Melchizedek's identity in the readings and won't give away my answer in this opening paragraph. What I will say, however, is that the question that dominated my thoughts as I wrote the book was not whether the king-priest in Genesis 14 was an Old Testament Christophany, but rather, what does he reveal about Jesus, and how does that affect how we live?

This book is based on the thesis that while God loves and wants to bless us all, His special blessings are reserved for those who have a close relationship with Him and who are living in a manner that pleases Him. God is by nature a blesser. Jesus Himself makes this clear when He says that God "makes His sun to rise on the evil and the good, and sends rain on the just and the unjust" (Matt. 5:45). But God's promises, unlike His love, are not unconditional; their fulfillment depends on how we respond.

To receive God's best blessings, we must have a relationship with Him. The closer this relationship is, the more lavishly can God bless us—and I don't mean just materially. Some of His best blessings are the ones we cannot see. But even intangible gifts such as wisdom and a deeper revelation of His love will affect the physical, temporal areas of life.

THE STORY BEHIND THE BOOK

Another question I have encountered relates to the book's backstory. What made you write about Melchizedek, people want to know. This is a question I love! Like most authors, I enjoy being asked how I came by my subject.

For years I had a vague, fuzzy knowledge of Melchizedek, and the truth of his importance dawned on me over a period of several months, culminating in a revelation that engulfed me so swiftly that I handwrote the book's outline in one day flat! But Melchizedek's name had been floating in and out of my thoughts constantly since that warm spring morning in 2015 when the Holy Spirit had prompted me to read Psalm 110.

As I began to study this psalm, I discovered two fascinating facts: it is the psalm most often quoted or alluded to in the New Testament; and it is the most messianic of all. Other parts of the Psalter are more explicitly messianic, foretelling incidents that will take place during Jesus' earthly life, but this one is *entirely* so. All seven verses are about the Messiah! Melchizedek is mentioned in verse 4, where David refers to the messianic king as "a priest forever according to the order of Melchizedek." His name next appears in Hebrews, again with reference to the priesthood of Jesus.

When the Holy Spirit prompted me to read Psalm 110, it was shortly after He had given me the first of the two insights that freed me from years of depression. I prayed David's prophetic words many times in the following months, little realizing that this was building up to a book. In His perfect time the Lord led me to write *The Blessing of Melchizedek*, and my study has deepened not only my understanding of Jesus' priestly ministry but also my love and gratitude.

Months before that warm spring morning when I read Psalm 110, I had already begun praying for a new book. During a trip to India I spent a couple weeks in Mussoorie, a hill station near my father's hometown of Dehradun, to seek the Lord more intentionally. One afternoon midway through the fortnight, I was sitting in a slanting shaft of sunshine in my hotel room when these seven words dropped into my mind: "*Your faith is more precious than gold.*"

I had no idea at the time that faith would be the theme of my new book. I simply took it as an exhortation to ask God to purify my faith. I had recently expressed grave doubts about whether I would ever be healed of depression and other longstanding medical conditions, and I had been sensing that unless something shifted I was on the brink of a crisis of faith. The seven words that had just dropped into my mind were from 1 Peter 1:7, which tells us that our faith is "much more precious than gold that perishes, though it is tested by fire."

My thoughts drifted to 1993 and the first major crisis of my adulthood, when the Lord had promised to make me a woman of faith. Back then He had spoken to me through the same verse and used the same analogy of gold being refined in the furnace to show me the purpose of that trial, and in response I had asked Him to purify my faith of its dross. Now, all these years later in Mussoorie, I once again made the prayer I had made as a young woman so long ago.

When the shaft of sunshine sloped away, I left the room for a walk. The road outside the hotel had a commanding view of the

Himalayas, far across the span of many valleys. On another day I would have stood and gazed at the snows glittering in the afternoon light, but today I barely glanced in their direction as I marched along briskly. My whole focus was on what God had said about my faith. As I meditated on those words from 1 Peter, I got the impression that I must stop praying for a new book and spend the rest of my time in Mussoorie praying for my faith to be renewed.

I did not like that impression at all! I had set aside this fortnight specifically to seek God for a new book. In fact, God Himself had led me to make the trip, and He had told me what to pray for even before I boarded the train to Dehradun. I was sure that if I persevered in prayer He would give me a new book. On the other hand, I also knew I must obey what He was *now* telling me to do. The walk of faith, like any walk, has its bends and turns, and keeping in step with God is more than a matter of walking in a straight line. It means turning when He directs, though we may not know what lies around the bend.

I continued up the circuitous road, wrestling with the choice before me. Apart from the weighty matter of obedience, I knew deep down that a new book with an infirm faith was ultimately futile. Even God's most special blessings are not more precious than our faith, for faith is the means by which we relate with God.

The decision I had to make that afternoon was a difficult one, and I could not have done it without the Lord's enabling grace. God always gives us the grace to obey Him if we are willing. And although it is often not easy, obedience makes life an adventure as nothing else can.

The renewing of my faith turned out to be one of the grandest adventures of my life. That it was so closely connected with the new book I had prayed for—and then *stopped* praying for—

was just one of those spectacular surprises our heavenly Father loves springing upon His children.

HOW TO USE THIS DEVOTIONAL

We will explore the blessing of Melchizedek at three levels: literal, metaphorical, and typological. The first is the actual historical story which, like any story, has its unique context, plot, and cast of characters. And since Melchizedek's blessing is metaphorical of what God has for us, at the second level he represents God and Abraham represents us. The third level explores Melchizedek as a type of Christ. It will be helpful to keep these three levels in mind while reading this devotional.

Although Melchizedek is the titular hero, the dramatic hero is Abraham, the man to whom the action happens. This action includes events such as the famous call that opens Genesis 12 and the rescue of Lot, both of which precede the meeting with Melchizedek. I have also examined why Abraham has gone down in history as the father of all who believe.

Abraham is a heavyweight among heavyweights. No other character so closely typifies the Father who sacrificed His only Son, and no one else teaches us more about how to inherit God's promises. God made some lavish promises to Abraham, and he inherited them through faith, patience, and obedience.

In Christ we too have been given "exceedingly great and precious promises" (2 Pet. 1:4) and been blessed with "every spiritual blessing in the heavenly places" (Eph. 1:3). God also has special, specific blessings for each of us—things that can transform our lives here on earth and produce fruit that will endure throughout eternity. As Jesus says in John 15:16, He has appointed us to bear "fruit that will last" (NIV). Thus, *the blessed life is the fruitful life,* and we obtain it the same way that Abraham did: through faith, patience, and obedience.

Don't feel discouraged if you are not there yet. God is gracious and rich in mercy, and He wants you to receive His special blessings even more than you want them! If you are a member of His family, fruitfulness and favor are your inheritance. Whatever has been your history, it will not determine your destiny if today you will choose to draw near to God and live in a manner that pleases Him.

Whether you are a new Christian or you have been a follower of Jesus for years, this devotional is for you. It will show you both *what* God has for you and *how* you can obtain it. And since we master any skill by doing it, over the course of the 100 days you will also build up your devotional life by actually *doing* it. It doesn't matter if you've never had a devotional life, or if you once had one and it has fizzled out. What matters is that God is extending an invitation to you today.

Bear in mind as you read that you are only seeing a piece of the puzzle every day. The goal of the 100-day format is to build your devotional life incrementally. Just as we become physically fit with many consecutive workouts, not by one long session, so also we develop our devotional life over a period of time. For this reason I recommend that you not go through several readings in one sitting. If you miss a day, don't try to make up by reading two the next day. The point is not to accumulate information but to *acquire a habit*.

I'm aware that the method I am prescribing—doing one devotion daily, and not reading more than one a day—may not always be easy to follow. If you're wondering how you will manage to do this consistently, remember that God's mercies are new every morning (Lam. 3:22–23), and the grace of our Lord Jesus Christ is available and sufficient for every need (2 Cor. 12:9). All you have to do is ask and receive.

Each reading concludes with a devotional exercise comprising a New Testament chapter for further reading, a scripture for reflection, and a suggestion for prayer. The books are not in biblical sequence, but you will read each straight through. (The only exception is Romans, from which I took only eleven chapters so as to fit the 100-day format.) The chapters may not speak directly to the reading they follow, but the books I have selected speak to the subject as a whole.

Before you begin, invite the Holy Spirit to speak to you through the chapter, then read it slowly. For the purposes of this exercise, you are not reading simply to find out what the chapter says but *what God wants to say to you through it*. Even though you may have read it many times before, God has something new to say to you *today*, and that's what you're seeking. You may want to keep a notebook handy, to record what He says. (Sentences and paragraphs are not necessary. Words and phrases count too!)

Unlike the New Testament chapter, the reflection verse is directly related to the reading. It is a gift for you to take into your day. Meditate on it as you go about your tasks. As you do, the Lord will give you unfolding insights into His Word. If you incline your heart to hearing His voice, God will surely speak to you. And as with any meaningful conversation, *you* must speak to *Him*.

After reading the scripture, pray as suggested, and keep praying throughout the day. (Here I *do* recommend sentences and paragraphs!) Just as we can terminate a human conversation when we stop listening or speaking, we can do the same to our conversation with God. But the One who spoke the universe into existence wants to engage you in the most stimulating conversation you'll ever have—*one that need never end*—so keep listening and speaking to Him.

The prayer points are along the lines of asking the Holy Spirit to show you how to apply the content to your life. This pattern will allow you to develop a habit of hearing and obeying His voice. The suggestions may seem repetitive, even simplistic at times, but don't let that put you off. Learning any skill requires repetition, and mastering a skill always involves *mastering the basics*.

Wherever you are in your relationship with the Lord, you are embarking on a grand adventure as you start this devotional. Use it in the manner prescribed, relying on Christ's enabling grace to help you, and choose to trust and obey Him daily. If you do, you'll be transformed at the end of the 100 days. And since the fruitful life springs from the devotional life, you will find that the end is just the beginning.

Prologue

A PROMISE OF BLESSING

I have set before you life and death, blessing and curses. Now choose life, so that you and your children may live and that you may love the LORD your God, listen to his voice, and hold fast to him. For the LORD is your life.

—DEUTERONOMY 30:19–20 NIV

My son, do not forget my teaching, but keep my commands in your heart, for they will prolong your life many years and bring you peace and prosperity. Blessed are those who find wisdom, those who gain understanding, for she is more profitable than silver and yields better returns than gold. She is a tree of life to those who take hold of her; those who hold her fast will be blessed.

—PROVERBS 3:1–2,13–14,18 NIV

Whatever we ask we receive from Him, because we keep His commandments and do those things that are pleasing in His sight.

—1 JOHN 3:22

Fruitful Days
1–3

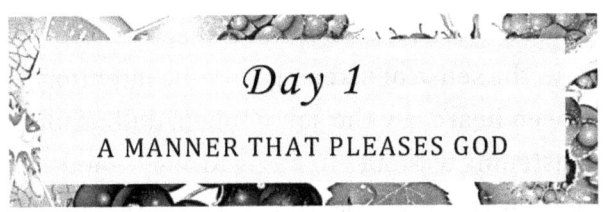

Day 1
A MANNER THAT PLEASES GOD

The blessing of Melchizedek is the first instance in Scripture of one person speaking a blessing over another. When the story is read at the literal level, as an actual historical event, it reminds us that we must aspire to always bless others, by our actions and also by our words. But since Melchizedek is typological of Christ, and since he represents God at the metaphorical level, his blessing speaks even more distinctly of God's eagerness to bless us.

As noted in the introduction, *The Blessing of Melchizedek* is based on the thesis that God's special blessings are reserved for those who have a close relationship with Him and who are living in a manner that pleases Him. Abraham is the most prominent example of such a person, but he is not the only one. Scripture is filled with people who responded to God's word in the right manner and thereby obtained what God had promised them.

Like Abraham, many of these biblical characters were promised things that humanly speaking could not happen; and like him, many of them were promised their blessing long before they received it. In the interim, they had to believe *and keep on believing* what God had said, and to wait patiently for Him to fulfill His word. In addition, they had to live in continual obedience, both to God's general instructions as well as to the specific directions He gave them in each situation.

The Hebrew word for obey, *shama*, means *to hear intelligently*. It conveys the sense of listening with the intention of obeying what has been heard. By the same token, dull or unintelligent hearing is listening without intending to obey—and according to God's definition, that is not hearing at all. For God, hearing is synonymous with obedience.

Hearing is also closely linked with faith. In Romans 10:17 we read that faith comes by hearing the word of God. The Greek word Paul uses twice in this verse, *akoe*, refers to inner spiritual hearing and discerning God's voice. And *rhema*, the word for word, refers to what is spoken by a living voice, particularly by *God's* voice. The *rhema* is a specific word given for a specific situation. It will never contradict the written Word, and obeying it will draw us closer to the Incarnate Word, our Lord Jesus. As God's people, our supreme goal should be to live under the sound of His voice through faith and obedience.

One of the Bible's most popular verses says, "We know that in all things God works for the good of those who love him, who have been called according to his purpose" (Rom. 8:28 NIV). From this verse we learn that God does three things: He sets the purpose; He calls; and He works all things for our good. We have to do only one thing, and that is to love Him. And as any parent knows, love is best demonstrated through faith and obedience.

READ: Hebrews 1
REFLECT: Romans 8:28
PRAY: Thank the Lord that He wants to bless you and ask Him to join you on this 100-day journey.

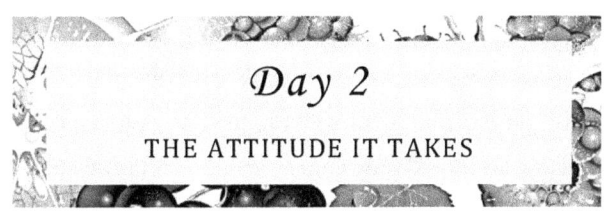

Day 2

THE ATTITUDE IT TAKES

Melchizedek's blessing opens with the word *baruk*, which is a participle of the verb *barak*. One of the primary meanings of this verb is *to bend the knee* or *to kneel down*.

Kneeling is an appropriate posture both for receiving a blessing from someone and for showing honor to them, and this is especially true with respect to honoring God and receiving His blessing. Kneeling implies an attitude of humility, and it takes humility to receive anything, blessing included. Moreover, the image of a person being on their knees reminds us that God's blessing must result *from* and *in* worship.

The Hebrew noun for blessing, *berakah*, implies benediction, benefit, favor, and peace. It can also refer to a gift given to obtain someone's goodwill.

Psalm 2, the first messianic piece in the Psalter, closes with the injunction to "kiss the Son" (v. 12). To kiss the Son is to give Him the honor and blessing He is due as the Anointed of the Lord, the One who has the nations for His inheritance and the ends of the earth for His possession, as verse 8 says. The opening line of verse 12—"Kiss the Son, lest He be angry"—can only be fully understood when we read it together with the last, which tells us that *all who put their trust in the Son are blessed.*

Similar to *berakah* is *berekah*, which is a reservoir where camels kneel as a resting-place. The word conjures the image of a person being welcomed after a tiring journey with a cool, refreshing drink. To a large extent, this is what Melchizedek's blessing did for Abram when he returned from the slaughter of the kings.

The first time we encounter the word blessed in the Bible, it is when God blesses the first living creatures on the fifth day of Creation (Gen. 1:22). And fittingly, the first instance in the New Testament comes from the lips of our Lord: *blessed* is the opening word of the Sermon on the Mount (Matt. 5:3).

Prior to this, we have heard Jesus speak four times—at the Jordan, when He comes to be baptized; in the wilderness, when He counters each of the devil's temptations by quoting from the Torah; in Capernaum, where He preaches that the kingdom of heaven is at hand; and by the Sea of Galilee, when He calls the first disciples. The Sermon on the Mount is thus the fifth time we hear Jesus speak in the New Testament. That it opens with the word blessed is significant, because in the Bible the number five represents grace or unmerited favor, and favor, in essence, is what blessing is.

READ: Hebrews 2
REFLECT: Psalm 22:27–28
PRAY: Since Jesus has the nations for His inheritance, pray that the gospel will be freely preached in your nation.

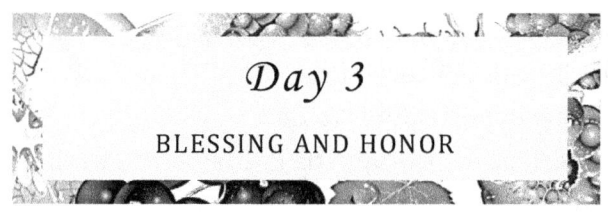

Day 3
BLESSING AND HONOR

The Hebrew word for peace, *shalom*, can be used in greeting as well as in farewell, and the Jewish concept of blessing is the same. Apart from the sense of greeting or welcome, it is also a benediction for what lies ahead, saying something to the effect of "May your journey go well," or "May all go well with you." It is similar to the Greek word for prosper, *euodoo* (used famously in 3 John 1:2), which means to have a happy or successful journey. As such, the Jewish concept of blessing resembles the Indian concept of *ashirwad*.

Young people in the land of my birth are taught the importance of seeking blessings from their elders, especially when they are on the threshold of something major like an exam or a job interview. This is typically done by touching the elders' feet and displaying other marks of respect, such as answering questions, listening to advice, and not declining the offer of chai. The blessing may not help if one hasn't studied for the exam or isn't qualified for the job, but my point is that the Indian culture understands the significance of obtaining blessing from those with greater wisdom, experience, and honor.

The elders whose blessing we are to desire most are our parents, and the best way we can do this is by honoring them. "Honor your father and mother" (Ex. 20:12) is the fifth of the Ten Commandments. That it immediately follows those pertaining to our relationship with God, even preceding "Thou shalt not murder," suggests how important it is to God.

In Ephesians 6:2 the apostle Paul reminds us that the commandment to honor our parents is the first with a promise. The Torah contains many commandments apart from the Ten, and most of them have promises attached, but this is *the first* with a promise. And where the Ten are concerned, it is the *only* commandment with a promise.

God means what He says. When He says "that it will go well with you," He means "that it will go well with you." The promise is stupendous! It tells us that when we honor our father and mother, the two people because of whom we have life, our life will go well. Conversely, the consequences of disobeying this command are equally sweeping. I have learnt this the hard way—but I can also testify that the Lord will always teach us what pleases Him and give us the grace to obey if we are willing.

Biblical obedience is an act of faith. We will explore this further as we study the blessing of Melchizedek in the days ahead, but if I had to summarize the message of this book in one sentence it would be this: *If we want what God has for us, we must obtain it His way.*

READ: Hebrews 3
REFLECT: Exodus 20:12
PRAY: Ask God to forgive you if you did not honor your parents and thank Him for them.

Part One

THE CONTEXT

The king of Sodom went out to meet [Abram] at the Valley of Shaveh (that is, the King's Valley), after his return from the defeat of Chedorlaomer and the kings who were with him. Then Melchizedek king of Salem brought out bread and wine; he was the priest of God Most High. And he blessed him.

—GENESIS 14:17–19

Be strong in the Lord and in the power of His might. Put on the whole armor of God, that you may be able to stand against the wiles of the devil. For we do not wrestle against flesh and blood, but against spiritual hosts of wickedness in the heavenly places. Therefore take up the whole armor of God.

—EPHESIANS 6:10–13

Imitate those who through faith and patience inherit the promises. For when God made a promise to Abraham, because He could swear by no one greater, He swore by Himself. And so, after he had patiently endured, he obtained the promise.

—HEBREWS 6:12–13,15

Fruitful Days
4–18

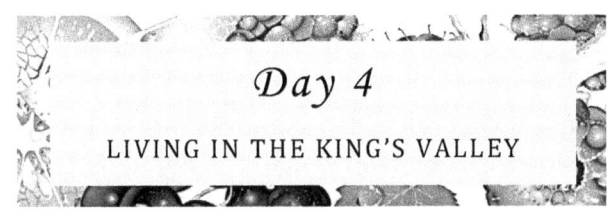

Day 4
LIVING IN THE KING'S VALLEY

The blessing of Melchizedek takes place in the Valley of Shaveh. The parenthetical clause in Genesis 14:17—"that is, the King's Valley"—is not a translation of Shaveh, because *shaveh* means a plain or field. Rather, the parenthetical clause is giving us a nickname or sobriquet.

Whatever the origin of the sobriquet, the King's Valley is a fitting place for Abram to be blessed by Melchizedek, who is not only king of Salem but who also prefigures the King of kings, our Lord Jesus Christ. This suggests that for the Valley of Shaveh to be the place of blessing, it must be the *King's* Valley. It must be the place where the King is present, because God's presence is a prerequisite for His blessing. Even in the midst of trouble and trials, God is willing to bless us *if we will welcome His presence*. We do this primarily through worship, and also by repenting of any sin the Holy Spirit might reveal. Sin is the surest way of keeping God's holy presence at bay, and repentance is the surest way of bringing it back.

The Valley of Shaveh may be a valley, but that does not affect or limit the blessing. We sometimes think that God can bless us only on the mountaintops, in times when we are soaring spiritually, but here we see our spiritual ancestor being blessed in a *valley*. Valleys are geologically low areas, and they typify times of distress and even depression. But Abram's meeting with Melchizedek in the King's Valley reminds us that wherever the King is present, we may expect His blessing. The key is in recognizing that God's blessings are not always material and tangible, and they don't always look like blessings when we first encounter them.

Blessings often come in disguise. They don't always come dressed as themselves, and only a truly discerning person will see them for what they are. For instance, if distress or lack throws us more fully into worship and study of the Word, then that is a blessing. If we are willing to see a trial as a blessing in disguise, God can use it to increase in us qualities such as wisdom, humility, patience, and trust—qualities that not only bless us but also make us a blessing to others. Everything depends on how we view what comes our way, and whether we are willing to let God do His will in any circumstance. This is how a valley can become a place of blessing.

The name Joseph gave his second son, Ephraim, means fruitfulness, for he said, "God has caused me to be fruitful in the land of my affliction" (Gen. 41:52). The fruitfulness God had for Joseph would bless the entire ancient world, but he had to be prepared for it in a dungeon. His unjust imprisonment matured him to the extent that he could assume the position of Pharaoh's right-hand man with wisdom and grace. Among the many things we learn from the life of Joseph is that we can find fruitfulness in and even *through* affliction.

> *READ: Hebrews 4*
> *REFLECT: Psalm 23:4*
> *PRAY: Think of one "blessing in disguise" in your life and ask the Lord to show you how He wants to use it.*

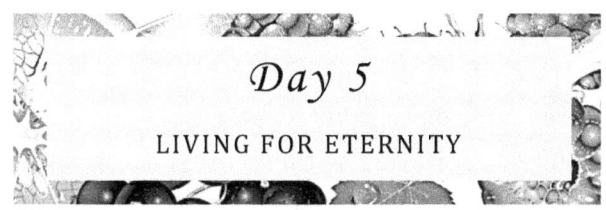

Day 5

LIVING FOR ETERNITY

After Genesis 14, the King's Valley is mentioned only once more in the Bible. In 2 Samuel 18:18 it is referred to as the place where David's favorite son erected a monument for himself. Absalom did this because he had no sons to carry on his name, little realizing that biological offspring and stone pillars are not the real memorials. The memorials that will last for eternity are our own lives —if they are lived by faith. "Whatever is not from faith is sin," says Paul in Romans 14:23; and since whatever is of sin will be destroyed, the apostle is saying that whatever is not from faith *will not count for eternity.*

The most profound thing ever said on living for eternity came from the lips of our Lord Himself:

> Do not store up for yourselves treasures on earth, where moth and rust destroy and where thieves break in and steal, but store up for yourselves treasures in heaven. . . . For where your treasure is, there your heart will be also. (Matt. 6:19–21 ESV)

This tells us that living for heaven is a matter of where our heart is *while we are still on earth.* When we seek first the kingdom of God and His righteousness, as Jesus instructs in Matthew 6:33, we are storing up treasures for ourselves in heaven. Then, when we die we will go *to* our treasure, not away from it. If our treasures are here on earth, when we die we will leave them behind. And since we are destined to die only once (Heb. 9:27), we will never return to our earthly treasures.

Unlike his father David and their ancestor Abraham, Absalom did not live for eternity, because he did not cultivate a love for God's presence as they did. On the contrary, his story is one of pride, brutality, and gross sin. When his sister Tamar is raped by their half-brother Amnon, Absalom takes matters into his own hands to avenge the crime and has Amnon killed. Now the sin of incest is compounded by the sin of murder, and it exacerbates David's grief.

Three years later, when David allows Absalom to return to Jerusalem, he says, "Let him return to his own house, but do not let him see my face" (2 Sam. 14:24). Since the king was God's representative, his face was symbolic of the face of God, and the face of God stands for His favor. Thus, by not allowing Absalom to see his face, David was inflicting upon his favorite son a severe though justly deserved punishment.

Ironically, even though his name means *the father is peace*, Absalom was perpetually at war with his father and he died a rebel in battle. Whenever Absalom's name is spoken, posterity remembers a man who rebelled against his father. Nothing of the monument he erected in the King's Valley remains, but his life and death serve as an example of how *not* to live. That has become his legacy.

READ: Hebrews 5
REFLECT: Matthew 6:21
PRAY: Ask the Lord to show you one way you can invest in eternity today.

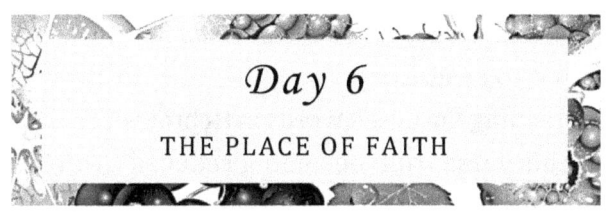

Day 6

THE PLACE OF FAITH

Shaveh is a plain, and a plain is a level stretch of land. The straight, even topography of Shaveh evokes a state of moral straightness, uprightness, and integrity. As Isaiah 26:7 says, "The path of the righteous is level" (ESV). Abram is an upright man, and he is known as the father of all who believe (Rom. 4:11). Since faith is his defining quality, the Valley of Shaveh can also be seen as the place of faith.

Faith is holding something to be true, and biblical faith is holding *what the Bible says* to be true. Hebrews 11, the faith chapter of the Bible, opens with this well-known definition of faith: "Now faith is the substance of things hoped for, the evidence of things not seen."

The definition in Hebrews 11:1, while it is succinct and memorable, has two drawbacks. The first is overfamiliarity. Many of us have heard it so often that it has become a cliché, and clichés elicit boredom and indifference.

The second limitation—at least in English—is that the words substance and evidence in the NKJV (translated *confidence* and *assurance* in other versions) are abstract nouns. Abstract nouns, as the name suggests, refer to things that are not concrete. These terms can thus reduce faith to an idea, whereas biblical faith is actually an *action*. The word faith may be a noun in the dictionary, but in actual experience it is a *verb*. We *do* faith. The primary action of faith is to *believe*.

Understanding the Greek words in Hebrews 11:1 will keep the subject of this verse from becoming reduced to an idea. *Hupostasis*, the word for substance, literally means *standing under a guaranteed agreement* and can refer to the title deed to a property. That's how tangible biblical faith is! And *elegchos*, the word for evidence, not only means conviction but also *the charge or proof* by which someone is convicted. Thus faith is as real and reliable as a piece of evidence that can be proved in a court of law.

We rarely encounter the noun faith in the Old Testament. The more common Hebrew word is the verb *aman*, meaning to confirm or support. Among its various meanings are trust, believe, and have assurance. From this root we get the adverb *amen*, meaning verily or truly, and the noun *emunah*, meaning firmness, stability, steadfastness, and fidelity.

This important word *emunah* first appears in Exodus 17:12, where Aaron and Hur hold up Moses' hands so they remain steady until sunset. The result is that the Amalekites, the first enemies Israel faced in the wilderness, are completely defeated. The usage suggests that steadfast, unshakeable faith produces victory. As 1 John 5:4 says, "This is the victory that has overcome the world, *even our faith*" (NIV).

READ: Hebrews 6
REFLECT: Hebrews 11:1
PRAY: Think of one area in which you need victory and ask the Lord to give you overcoming faith in this area.

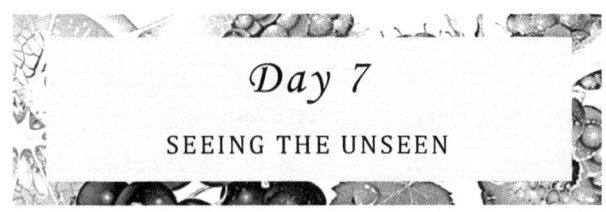

Day 7

SEEING THE UNSEEN

"Not seen" is a critical part of the definition in Hebrews 11:1. Faith is not sight, but it leads to sight, and as believers we are to "live by faith, not by sight" (2 Cor. 5:7 NIV).

Often in the Gospels we find people believing in Jesus after they witness a miracle, and our Lord Himself acknowledges this. When Philip asks, "Lord, show us the Father and that will be enough for us," Jesus replies, "Believe in me when I say that I am in the Father and the Father is in me; *or at least* believe in the evidence of the works themselves" (John 14:11 NIV).

The works testify to Jesus' identity, but faith that needs the evidence of the works is of a less mature kind, as implied by the phrase "or at least." The greater faith is that which believes in God's *word*, which is why in the verses before and after this one Jesus mentions *"the words that I speak to you"* and *"I say to you"* (John 14:10,12).

We find Jesus saying something similar earlier in John's Gospel, just before He performs one of His greatest miracles, the raising of Lazarus. When He commands that the stone be removed, Martha squeamishly protests about the stench, for her brother has been dead four days. Jesus has just given her the ultimate revelation of Himself—*"I am the resurrection and the life"*—but it's going to take a miracle for it to sink in.

Instead of chiding Martha for her oversensitive nose, Jesus goes straight to the heart of the matter: her under-sensitive faith. He says, "Did I not say to you if you would believe you would see the glory of God?" (John 11:40). After this, He says the word and Lazarus comes forth, and everyone sees the glory of God.

Believing God's word before we see His work is true faith. In Genesis 15:6, the first instance where a person's faith is credited to them as righteousness, it is because Abram believes what God has just *said* to him. He is yet to have a single child, but the Lord has said that his descendants will be numberless as the stars in the sky, and God's word is good enough for the man of faith.

Faith is ultimately a positive response to God. It involves both belief and behavior. It both *believes* certain things about God, and *does* certain things in response to that knowledge.

The Bible contains numerous cases of people who displayed a positive response to God. Among the first in the New Testament is the Roman centurion who tells Jesus, "Just say the word, and my servant will be healed" (Matt. 8:8 NIV). Jesus commends this as "great faith," and it is one of only two things that amaze Him. The only other time the verb *thaumazo*, meaning to be astonished or amazed, is used of Jesus is people's *lack* of faith (Mark 6:6).

If we want to amaze our Lord, we can choose either response, faith or lack of faith, but only one will lead to blessing.

READ: Hebrews 7
REFLECT: John 11:40
PRAY: Think of an area where your response to God needs to be more positive and ask Him to help you change.

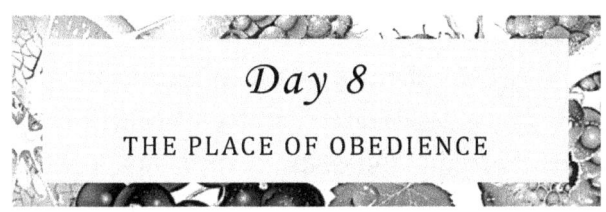

Day 8

THE PLACE OF OBEDIENCE

Abram would not have reached the Valley of Shaveh without faith and obedience. His meeting with Melchizedek was preceded by many previous acts of faith, acts reflected in obedience. For instance, as the writer of Hebrews says, "By faith Abraham obeyed when he was called to go out to the place which he would receive as an inheritance" (Heb. 11:8). The Greek word for obeyed in this verse, *hupakouo*, conveys the sense of attentively listening to the one giving orders. Thus it resembles the Hebrew verb *shama*, which means *to hear with the intention of obeying*, as we noted on Day 1.

Everything about our relationship with God is based on faith, and obedience is among the surest signs of faith. We may *claim* we have faith, but until we actually do what God requires, we cannot *prove* it. In the legal system, filing a claim does not guarantee a favorable verdict unless there is evidence to prove that the claim is valid.

The legal systems of the world can be corrupt, so that valid claims are denied and vice versa, but God's court of law is perfectly and consistently just. As the psalmist has declared, "Righteousness and justice are the foundation of Your throne" (Ps. 89:13). When our claim to faith is supported by the evidence of obedience, it will accepted as valid.

God has given us His general commands in His Word, and we are expected to obey them if we are in a covenant relationship with Him. He also gives us directions for specific situations. These words never contradict the written Word, and only the Spirit of God can reveal them to us. It might be something big, like "Leave this city and move to this other city," or something smaller, like "Ask your sister to forgive you for what you said."

Where faith comes in—in the big things and the small—is trusting that what God is telling us to do will ultimately work out for our good. The fear that obeying God will bring ill is the devil's lie. Only *disobedience* brings ill. Following our own inclinations might be easy and pleasurable for a while, but it eventually leads to heartache and loss. Anyone who has knowingly disobeyed God knows this. Obedience, by contrast, works out for good, even if it may take time.

God usually reveals His specific will incrementally. He often gives us a vision for our lives early on, but the details get revealed *as we live*. Life is lived out one choice at a time—and at times we make the *wrong* choices. In such cases, God has to work with those choices as well. He can redeem any mistake, but a wrong choice means that God must bring us back on course, just as a missed turn while we are driving means we must turn around or take a detour to reach our destination.

READ: Hebrews 8
REFLECT: Luke 11:28
PRAY: Ask the Lord to show you one unrepented act of disobedience and ask Him to forgive and restore you.

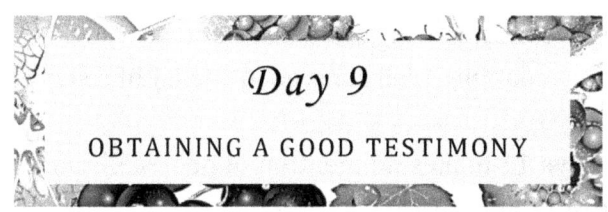

Day 9

OBTAINING A GOOD TESTIMONY

Sandwiched between the definition that opens Hebrews 11 and the faith hall of fame, which fills the rest of the chapter, is a brief, overlooked verse. It is often dwarfed by the glorious material surrounding it, but where inheriting the promises is concerned, it is the *key* verse of the Bible's faith chapter: "For by [faith] the elders obtained a good testimony" (Heb. 11:2).

Some versions say the elders received commendation or approval by their faith. These are more literal translations of *emartyrethesan*, which derives from the verb *martureo*, meaning to bear witness, give evidence, testify, and give a good report. But the NKJV's "obtained a good testimony" anticipates Revelation 12:11, where the word of our testimony is named as one of the ways we overcome the accuser.

The word obtain derives from the Latin *obtinere*, meaning to take hold of, hold on to, or possess. This aptly depicts what faith allows us do to God's promises. The Greek verb *kleronomeo*, which means to acquire or to obtain by inheritance, is used in Hebrews 6:12, where we are told to "imitate those who through faith and patience inherit the promises."

When we combine these various translations, a clear picture emerges of what God has for us. We are to have a good testimony during our lifetime, we must strive to leave behind a legacy of faith, and we must live in such a manner that we will earn God's final commendation, "Well done, good and faithful servant" (Matt. 25:21).

Hebrews 11 makes no mention of people obtaining wealth and ease by their faith. On the contrary, we find that their faith led them to *give up* riches, comforts, and other privileges. By faith Abel offered a better sacrifice, and he lost his life for it. By faith Noah built an ark in full view of a wicked and violent generation. By faith Moses left the treasures of Egypt and the pleasures of sin to suffer with God's people.

The unnamed heroes referred to at the end of the faith hall of fame were tortured, had "trial of mockings and scourgings," were stoned to death, sawn in two, and slain by the sword. They wandered in deserts and dens, "being destitute, afflicted, tormented" (Heb. 11:35–38). This hardly resembles the contemporary idea of a good testimony, and yet that's exactly how the Bible puts it.

Earlier in the epistle, the writer had reminded us that nothing in creation is hidden from God's sight: "Everything is uncovered and laid bare before the eyes of him to whom we must give an account" (Heb. 4:13 NIV). This is a powerful motivator for anyone who wants to obtain a good testimony. Knowing that we will one day have to give an account compels us to live by faith and obedience. And the knowledge that God sees everything enables us to wait patiently, confident that at the right time we will receive what has been promised.

READ: Hebrews 9
REFLECT: Hebrews 11:2
PRAY: Ask the Lord to help you obtain a good testimony in one area today—even if it is an area others cannot see.

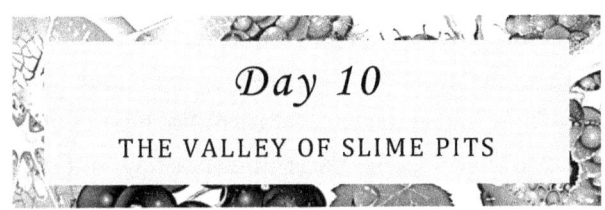

Day 10

THE VALLEY OF SLIME PITS

The blessing of Melchizedek follows the first war mentioned in the Bible, the Battle of the Vale of Siddim, also known as the war of the kings, and once again we encounter a parenthetical clause. The clause in Genesis 14:3—"that is, the Salt Sea"—is not a translation of the word *siddim*, which means *flats*. Rather, it is giving us the new name of the Vale of Siddim, which is the Salt Sea. As with the Valley of Shaveh, the geology of Siddim provides a clue to its spiritual significance.

Originally a fruitful valley abounding with orchards and gardens, the Vale of Siddim was paradoxically also full of asphalt pits. Asphalt or bitumen is a black, viscous form of petroleum. When it seeps to the earth's surface, its lighter elements vaporize and what remains is the thick, slimy residue that creates tar pits. Tar pits are a deathtrap for animals, and some of those fleeing the forces of Chedorlaomer king of Elam, the chief belligerent, meet the same fate.

The Vale of Siddim became the Salt Sea after the destruction of Sodom and Gomorrah. When God rained down fire and brimstone on these cities, the bituminous pits turned into a sulfurous lake that became known as the Salt Sea. Today we call it the Dead Sea, *dead* because of its inability to sustain life due to abnormally high salinity.

Apart from its name, certain other features of the Dead Sea make it a fitting location for the first war mentioned in the Bible. It is an endorheic lake—a closed or terminal basin with no means of draining into the sea. The water does not flow out as it should; it can only escape by evaporation or seepage. Furthermore, at 1,400 feet below sea level, the Dead Sea is the lowest elevation on earth's surface, which recalls the moral depravity of Sodom and Gomorrah.

At the metaphorical level, the Vale of Siddim represents regions of spiritual darkness, where the forces of wickedness are most active. Just as Abram was spared from becoming involved in the war until the very end, the Lord will protect us from the Siddims that surround us if we remain under His protection. But since we live in a world where wickedness is rife, at times we will have to engage in spiritual warfare, just as Abram could not avoid getting involved in the war.

The war of the kings took place during the reign of Amraphel king of Shinar (Gen. 14:1). Amraphel is the first person to be called a king in the Bible, and Shinar is the first kingdom (Gen. 10:10). Founded by Nimrod, grandson of Noah's dishonorable son Ham, Shinar's chief city was Babel, site of the doomed tower. The city was later renamed Babylon, and its final fall will take place in the day of the Lord, as we learn from Revelation 18. Thus the first war in the Bible seems to foreshadow the last.

READ: Hebrews 10
REFLECT: Ephesians 6:10
PRAY: Think of one area of your life that is under attack and ask the Lord to show you how to resist the devil.

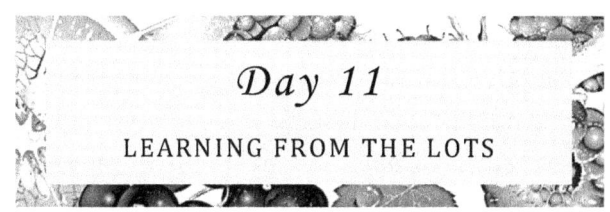

Day 11

LEARNING FROM THE LOTS

Abram gets involved in the war of the kings because his nephew Lot is among those abducted by Chedorlaomer. Lot has been residing in Sodom since the strife between his herdsmen and Abram's, the incident in which we get the first mention of the word strife (Gen. 13:7).

When Abram suggests that they separate to resolve the strife, he graciously lets Lot choose where he will move, and Lot picks the best-looking place and pitches his tent as far as Sodom. His choice is based on what his eyes see, for he is attracted to what *looks* good. This is the defining trait of a person who lives by their flesh and not by the Spirit. Lot's decision also reflects selfishness, for he wants the best for himself.

Perhaps Lot had no idea that the men of Sodom were "exceedingly wicked and sinful against the LORD" (Gen. 13:13) when he moved there; but no doubt he found out afterwards, and he should have left. Centuries later the apostle Peter calls him "righteous Lot," saying he was "tormenting his righteous soul" over what he saw and heard (2 Pet. 2:7–8 ESV).

The point Peter was making was that "the Lord knows how to rescue the godly from trials" (v. 9), but my point is that *Lot could have avoided needing to be rescued in the first place*. He did not have to live among the people of Sodom and torment his soul day after day. Had he left when he discovered the truth, he would have bypassed the trial altogether. But Lot stayed put.

Lot stayed put because the land was pleasant and productive, because it would have been inconvenient to move again, and because he probably had the "to each his own" mentality. Let the people of Sodom do as they pleased, as long as it did not affect him or his family—but as it turns out, Sodom has corrupted all three women in Lot's family. His daughters get him drunk and seduce him, and his wife is foolish enough to disobey the angels' command to not look back as the Lord is destroying Sodom and Gomorrah.

Lot's wife lacked two things that would have helped her avoid death by crystallization. She lacked the will to obey, and she lacked the wisdom to recognize signs even when they were placed squarely in front of her. The Lord had sent two angels to their home on that fateful night, and the angels had even taken them by the hand and led them out of Sodom. What's more, *God was raining fire and brimstone from heaven.*

The most sobering part of this story is found in the one mention of Lot's wife in the New Testament. While talking about the Second Coming, Jesus says, "Remember Lot's wife" (Luke 17:32). It is the only time He tells us to remember someone, and He follows it up with a warning: "Whoever seeks to save his life will lose it, and whoever loses his life will preserve it."

READ: Hebrews 11
REFLECT: Luke 17:33
PRAY: Think of something you regret and ask the Lord to help you to stop looking back.

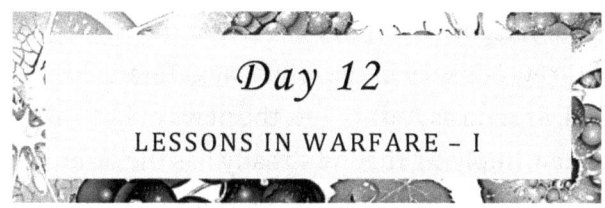

Day 12

LESSONS IN WARFARE - I

The rescue of Lot is among the least familiar bits of Abraham's life, but it contains some key lessons in spiritual warfare.

As followers of Christ we are constantly at war with our archenemy, the devil, who wants to thwart God's plans for us, to rob us of anything he can, and ultimately to end our lives prematurely. Jesus Himself has said, "The thief comes *only* to steal and kill and destroy" (John 10:10 NIV). But while satanic activity against us is an inevitable part of our existence on earth, there are seasons when it is intensified and we face heightened attack. This is what Abram's involvement in the war represents, when viewed metaphorically.

One of the things that Abram's rescue of Lot suggests is that Abram is willing and prepared. He may already have been aware of the battle underway, but he may not have been expecting to hear of Lot's capture. Whatever the case, he goes into action as soon as he gets the news. He is ready for battle at a moment's notice.

Abram's readiness is a reminder that we must train ourselves *before* we need to be in battle. We must be praying and worshiping regularly in order to pray and worship when we suddenly find ourselves in a context of spiritual warfare. Filling ourselves daily with God's Word allows us to know how to wield it against the adversary, as our Lord did in each of the three temptations the devil threw His way in the wilderness (Matt. 4:4,7,10).

Second, as soon as Abram gets the news of Lot's abduction, he arms his men, implying that he already has the armor necessary. Ephesians 6, the Bible's spiritual warfare chapter, tells us that we must put on the full armor of God. Wearing the various pieces Paul lists is a matter of lifestyle and relationship rather than something we ritualistically "put on" to give us the sense of feeling protected.

Our armor also includes things mentioned elsewhere in the New Testament, things such as fasting, worship, and the items listed in Revelation 12:11—the blood of the Lamb, the word of our testimony, and not loving our lives "so much as to shrink from death" (NIV). Apart from our physical life, we are to not love those areas that must be yielded to God daily—including our mind, will, emotions, and bodily desires. That's why Paul says the weapons of our warfare are "not carnal," and that we must bring "every thought into captivity to the obedience of Christ" (2 Cor. 10:4–5).

The name of Jesus is one of our most powerful weapons against the devil, but to use it effectively we must first have a relationship with Jesus. The case of the sons of Sceva in Acts 19 is a warning not to use our Lord's name in spiritual warfare without the prerequisite of relationship.

READ: Hebrews 12
REFLECT: Ephesians 6:11
PRAY: Ask God to show you where your spiritual armor may be weak and how to make it stronger.

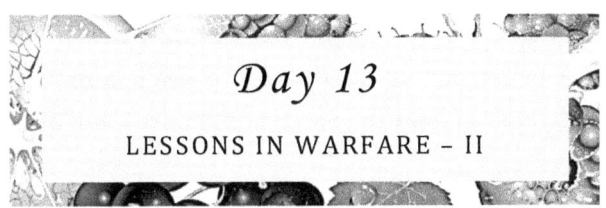

Day 13

LESSONS IN WARFARE - II

Genesis 14:14 tells us that Abram has 318 trained servants. At first it may seem strange to encounter so exact a number. Moses could have rounded it up or down, but he was writing under the guidance of the Holy Spirit, who clearly wanted to tell us something. For one thing, 318 is a large number and it speaks of how much God has already blessed Abram. For another, in some versions of the Bible the number five appears 318 times, and five, as we noted on Day 2, represents grace.

The Greek word for grace, *charis*, refers both to God's *unmerited favor*, by which we receive the gift of salvation, as well as His *enabling power*, by which we live in a manner that pleases Him.

Our entire life with Christ starts and ends with grace. We are saved by grace (Eph. 2:8), and we live by grace (2 Cor. 9:8). Therefore, we can only engage in spiritual warfare by His enabling, empowering grace. When Paul records Jesus' words about His grace being sufficient, he has just described the thorn in the flesh as "a messenger of Satan" (2 Cor. 12:7). This suggests that he may have been experiencing some sort of attack, and it is in this context that Jesus tells him, "My grace is sufficient for you" (v. 9).

Another lesson we can learn from the rescue of Lot is the importance of listening to the Holy Spirit. When Abram goes to war, he divides his forces by night, which indicates that he has a strategy. Since war is not his normal occupation, this can only mean that he has heard the voice of God. Abram is a man of prayer, which is why he can hear the voice of the Lord even as he is charging into battle.

We are warned to be vigilant because our enemy the devil prowls around "like a roaring lion, seeking whom he may devour" (1 Pet. 5:8). Vigilance does not mean that we are to be constantly on the lookout for the devil. Rather, we must be constantly *listening to the Holy Spirit*. We acquire this skill by shutting out other voices that clamor for our attention and by spending time in prayer and studying God's Word.

Listening also means that we ask the Holy Spirit specific questions and wait for Him to answer. While waiting, we must adopt an expectant attitude, resisting the temptation to doubt His love. We must also obey anything He tells us to do, even things not directly connected with what we are praying for, because obedience often speeds up the process. Conversely, disobedience always slows it down.

The Holy Spirit usually speaks in the still small voice that Elijah heard (1 Kings 19:12), and we can only hear it if we cultivate an ear for it. This comes by being attentive to Him in seemingly trivial everyday matters, gaining familiarity with His voice when the stakes are not high. Only then will we recognize it in the thick of battle.

READ: Hebrews 13
REFLECT: 2 Corinthians 12:9
PRAY: Ask the Lord for the grace to hear and obey His voice in at least one situation you will face today.

Day 14

THE FATHER'S BUSINESS

The blessing of Melchizedek occurs after the call of Abram in Genesis 12, which is the first major hinge point in the Bible. With this the narrative moves from the general history of humankind to the specific story of one man, and it's all leading up to the story of that man's greatest descendant.

When God calls Abram, He makes him some lavish promises, promises so lavish that posterity will refer to him as "the heir of the world" (Rom. 4:13). To fully appreciate how these promises shape Abram's future, and to understand the wider context of the blessing of Melchizedek, we must take a brief look at his past.

Abram was born in Ur of the Chaldees, an affluent Sumerian city on the Euphrates in southern Mesopotamia, and when God calls him he is living in Haran, a commercial and cultural center in Upper Mesopotamia. He is the firstborn of three brothers, the youngest of whom had died in Ur. His surviving brother Nahor is married to a woman named Milcah, and he himself is married to Sarai, who we later discover is his half-sister.

Abram's father Terah has descended from Noah's honorable son Shem, making him a Shemite (later *Semite*). The name Terah means *wandering*, and its bearer's life is tainted with spiritual wandering. His specific sin is idolatry. The Sumerian religion was polytheistic—at one point offering a choice of 3,600 deities—

and Terah seems to have taken his pick. Centuries later, the Lord will tell the Israelites, "Your fathers, *including Terah, the father of Abraham and the father of Nahor*, dwelt on the other side of the River in old times; and they served other gods" (Josh. 24:2).

It is believed that Terah was not only an idol worshipper but also an idol *maker*. Idol-making was lucrative in a land teeming with gods, and it is possible that Terah wanted his firstborn to inherit his business someday. God, on the other hand, wants Abram to inherit a different kind of family business, and it is described best by the greatest scion of his line.

Jesus is a boy of twelve when we first see Him without His earthly parents. As the family heads home after celebrating the Passover, Jesus lingers behind in Jerusalem. Joseph and Mary find Him three days later, dialoguing with the teachers in the Temple. "Son, why have You done this to us?" says Mary. "Your father and I have sought You anxiously" (Luke 2:48). Jesus replies, "Why did you seek Me? Did you not know that I must be about My Father's business?"

Chronologically, these are the first words we hear from the lips of Jesus. They tell us that even at that young age, He is absolutely sure about His identity and His destiny. He knows that He is the Son *of God*, and that the purpose of His life is to do His Father's business.

> READ: Matthew 1
> REFLECT: Romans 4:13
> PRAY: Thank the Lord for calling you into a relationship and ask Him to help you be about His business today.

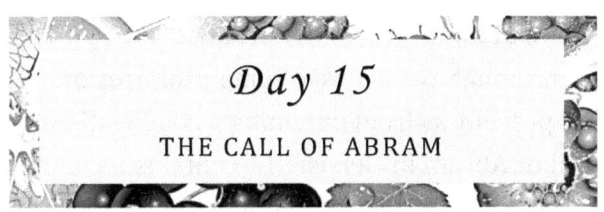

Day 15

THE CALL OF ABRAM

Life begins at seventy-five for Abram, when the Lord says to him,

> Get out of your country, from your family, and your father's house, to a land I will show you. I will make you a great nation; I will bless you and make your name great; and you shall be a blessing. I will bless those who bless you. And I will curse him who curses you; and in you all the families of the earth shall be blessed. (Gen. 12:1–3)

These pivotal verses reveal what God had for Abram; and Abram's response to the call teaches us how to obtain what God has for us. This response, as noted in the Introduction, can be summarized as faith, patience, and obedience.

With respect to what God has told him, Abram displays faith and obedience. With respect to time, the dimension in which the promises will be fulfilled, Abram responds with patience. This is why the writer of Hebrews exhorts us to "imitate those who through faith and patience inherit the promises" (Heb. 6:12), and he illustrates that statement through the example of Abraham.

Abraham died without receiving all that God had promised him because he was part of a story larger than his own. He "died in faith, without receiving the promises, but having seen them and welcomed them from a distance" (Heb. 11:13 NASB). As a matter of fact, *all* the elders, "having obtained a good testimony through faith, did not receive the promise" (v. 39). This teaches us that even though we may see some promises only from afar, it must not prevent us from obtaining a good testimony by faith.

The call of Abram in Genesis 12 contains a command and a promise. The command is that he must leave three things: his country, his family, and his father's house.

The country and the house may have been relatively easy to leave. Haran was not where he had grown up, and he probably had fewer close friends there than he did in Ur. Abram may also have been relieved to leave his father's house, being that of an idolater. But even so, a house is vastly more comfortable than a tent, and Abram probably understood that obeying God meant tent life for a while. As it turns out, it was tent life *for life*.

Separating from his family, even given Terah's idolatry, must have been harder for Abram than leaving the country and the house. We need only recall how he treats Lot to know how deeply Abram values family ties—and nor must we forget that Terah was also *Sarai's* father (Gen. 20:12). But leave they did, because Abram loved God enough to obey Him, and he had faith enough to take God at His word.

READ: Matthew 2
REFLECT: Hebrews 6:12
PRAY: Thank the Lord for His promises and ask Him to help you inherit them in the manner He has prescribed.

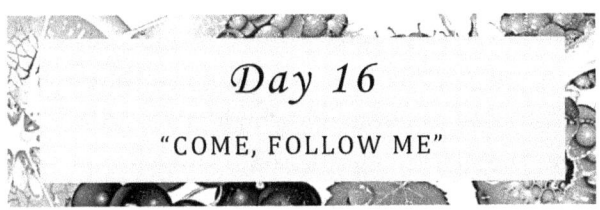

Day 16

"COME, FOLLOW ME"

The sevenfold promise that follows the threefold command is known as the Abrahamic covenant. The use of "I will" in God's statements implies that the good that will happen to and through Abram will be God's doing. And the final promise in the call—"in you all the families of the earth shall be blessed"—is the means by which Scripture "preached the gospel to Abraham beforehand" (Gal. 3:8), since it is a reference to the promised Messiah.

The command and the promise are not in equal measure: the latter is more than twice that of the former. The call of Abram is thus one of the earliest instances in Scripture of a key principle in the life of faith, that when God asks us to give up something, what He gives us in return is always far greater. As Jesus has promised,

> Everyone who has left houses or brothers or sisters or father or mother or wife or children or lands, for My name's sake, shall receive a hundredfold, and inherit eternal life. (Matt. 19:29)

The context of our Lord's statement is significant, for it follows the rich young ruler's visit. The man had come asking what he should do to inherit eternal life, and he left because he could not do what Jesus had said: "Sell what you have and give to the poor . . .; and come, follow Me" (Matt. 19:21).

Even though Jesus promises him treasure in heaven, the man is too tied to his earthly treasure to obey. Abram, by contrast, readily obeyed God's command, which proves that Abram knew God whereas the rich young ruler only knew the law. When Jesus had named the commandments he must keep, the man had bragged, "All these things I have kept from my youth" (Matt. 19:20).

Apart from promising him treasure in heaven, Jesus gives the rich young ruler the offer of a lifetime. *"Come, follow Me,"* He says, but the man rejects the offer. Thus, the most tragic difference between the rich young ruler and his forefather is that when God had told Abram *"Come, follow Me,"* Abram had seized the opportunity. His name has indeed become great, just as God promised, whereas we don't even know the rich young ruler's name. On the contrary, he has given the term "rich young ruler" a bad reputation, for it has come to epitomize someone who rejects Jesus because of their wealth.

Discipleship is the call to follow Jesus. We know this from Jesus' call to His very first disciples: *"Come, follow Me"* (Matt. 4:19). He promises to make the fishermen fishers of men, and they recognize that they are being offered the chance of a lifetime. At once they leave their nets and follow Jesus, just as their forefather Abraham had left everything to obey God's call.

> *READ: Matthew 3*
> *REFLECT: Matthew 19:29*
> *PRAY: Ask God to show you one thing that is keeping you from following Him fully and to help you change.*

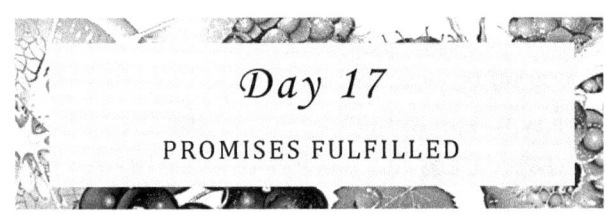

Day 17

PROMISES FULFILLED

By the time Abram received Melchizedek's blessing, God had already fulfilled *three* promises. The first was a "pre-promise," tucked away at the end of Genesis 12:1—*"to a land I will show you."* In response, Abram assembled his large household, and they "departed to go to the land of Canaan" (v. 5).

God had not mentioned any name in the call; He had simply said "to a land I will show you." So how did Abram know he must go to Canaan? He knew because God had promised to show him the place, and God always keeps His word.

According to Genesis 11:31, Canaan was Abram's destination *even before God called him out of Haran*. When Terah had left Ur of the Chaldees, he was actually heading for the land of Canaan, but for some reason he stopped at Haran and remained there for the rest of his life.

Whether Terah lacked the energy to continue, or whether he found some good prospects in Haran, or whether the name of the place, being similar to that of his dead son, motivated him to remain, we are not told. But one thing is clear: *God prevented the journey from progressing until the time was ripe for His promise.* Canaan was God's chosen destination for Abram, but it would have to come about as the result of His promise to Abram and Abram's response to that promise.

The first "promise proper" to be fulfilled was the word about cursing those who curse Abram (Gen. 12:3). This had happened back in Egypt, when Pharaoh took Sarai into his harem. God viewed this as an act of cursing, for He inflicted Pharaoh's household with "great plagues."

Pharaoh figures out that the plagues are connected with Sarai and he confronts Abram. He is perfectly justified in this—but then he brusquely sends Abram packing. He even commands his men to make sure Abram is driven out of Egypt. This is clearly not an act of blessing, and thus Pharaoh loses the chance of being blessed as Abimelech king of Gerar will later be. We are not told that Abraham ever prayed for Pharaoh's household or whether they recovered, whereas we are told that when Abraham prayed for Abimelech, "God healed Abimelech, his wife, and his female servants. Then they bore children" (Gen. 20:17).

The first thing we learn after the unceremonious expulsion from Egypt is that Abram was "very rich in cattle, in silver, and in gold" (Gen. 13:2). Pharaoh's treatment of Abram did not prevent God from fulfilling His promise to bless Abram, a truth we will do well to remember when we are surrounded by people who wish us ill. As David says of his enemies in Psalm 109, the best known of the imprecatory psalms, "Let them curse, but you will bless!" (v. 28 ESV).

> READ: Matthew 4
> REFLECT: Ephesians 1:3
> PRAY: Thank the Lord for one specific blessing you have as a follower of Jesus.

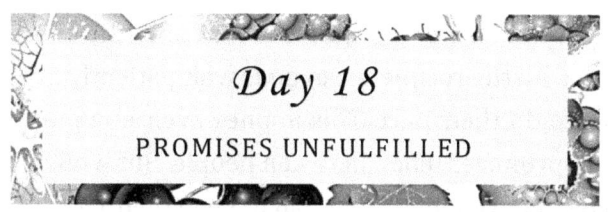

Day 18
PROMISES UNFULFILLED

The birth of Isaac is many years in the future when Abram meets Melchizedek. In Genesis 14, Abram is still a childless man. The word son might have pierced his heart whenever he heard or thought of it, yet we see Abram behaving righteously in this regard. He has not come up with a carnal plan to help God fulfill His promise, and nor has he acquired another wife because of Sarai's barrenness.

When God called Abram out of Haran, his brother Nahor was also childless. It is only after the Mount Moriah incident that Abraham learns that Milcah has borne children (Gen. 22: 20). The fact that Abraham is informed about Nahor's family so many decades after leaving Haran suggests that Milcah was also barren for a period. Yet only Sarai's barrenness is mentioned in Genesis 11, because only *her* barrenness is of consequence in God's redemptive story.

As it turns out, Sarai's barrenness is the *key* fact on which the story unfolds. The man is ageing, his wife is barren, and suddenly God shows up with the staggering promise that He will make them a great nation! It's a promise only God can fulfill—and this is true of all His promises, including His promises to us. *Only God can fulfill the promises He makes.*

The very nature of a promise is that only the one making it can fulfill it. All the recipient can do is wait patiently and trust the promiser to do their part. This applies even in a purely human context, to promises made between people. But while human beings may—and frequently do—fail to keep their word, God never does. Abraham's life is a case in point.

Descendants were not mentioned in the call, and we don't know if Abram suspected he would become a great nation through his own children, Sarai's barrenness notwithstanding, or through one of his servants. According to the inheritance laws of the day, a man could adopt a servant born in his house if he did not have a son of his own.

Having read the story we know that God will make Abram a great nation through Isaac, but God mentions descendants only *after* Abram departs Haran in obedience and by faith reaches Canaan. That's when God announces, "To your seed I will give this land" (Gen. 12:7).

Centuries later, after the Israelites had entered the Promised Land, their leader Joshua wrote, "Not a word failed of any good thing which the LORD had spoken to the house of Israel. All came to pass" (Josh. 21:43,45). Joshua could not have said this had God not kept His promise to give the land of Canaan to Abraham's descendants. And there would have been no "house of Israel" had God not first fulfilled His promise to give Abraham descendants.

> *READ: Matthew 5*
> *REFLECT: 1 Thessalonians 5:24*
> *PRAY: Think of one promise the Lord has fulfilled and thank Him for His faithfulness.*

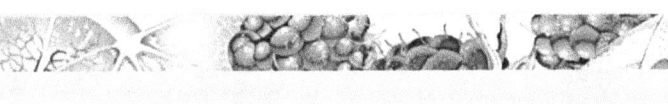

Part Two

THE KING

God created man in His own image, male and female He created them. Then God blessed them, and God said to them, "Be fruitful and multiply; fill the earth and subdue it; have dominion over the fish of the sea, over the birds of the air, and over every living thing that moves on the earth."

—GENESIS 1:27–28

In the beginning was the Word, and the Word was with God, and the Word was God. And the Word became flesh and dwelt among us, and we beheld His glory, the glory as of the only begotten of the Father, full of grace and truth.

—JOHN 1:1,14

Melchizedek, king of Salem, priest of the Most High God, who met Abraham returning from the slaughter of the kings and blessed him, to whom also Abraham gave a tenth part of the spoils, first being translated "king of righteousness," then also king of Salem, meaning "king of peace."

—HEBREWS 7:1–2

Fruitful Days
19–45

Day 19
THE KING

Names carry great weight in the Bible. A biblical character's name usually represented their destiny—specifically, what kind of person they would turn out to be. And more often than not, a person lived up to their name.

The name Melchizedek, meaning *king of righteousness*, is derived from *melek* (king) and *tsedeq* (righteousness). It comprises the names Melchi and Zadok, each of which sheds light on Melchizedek's character and what he reveals about Jesus.

The first part of Melchizedek's name points to God's kingship. Just as an earthly king is the sovereign ruler over his kingdom, God is the sovereign ruler over *His* kingdom. But unlike an earthly kingdom, which is obtained by conquest or through inheritance, the universe is God's kingdom by virtue of His having created it. We are told this in the very first verse of the Bible: "In the beginning, God created the heavens and the earth" (Gen. 1:1).

It takes faith to believe that God created the heavens and the earth. As the writer of Hebrews says, "*By faith* we understand that the worlds were framed by the word of God" (Heb. 11:3). We need faith to believe that the universe was created by God not because the biblical account is implausible but because we were not present when it happened, so we did not see it happen with our own eyes. For that same reason, it takes faith to believe *any* theory of the origin of the universe—but the biblical account and the other theories are mutually exclusive. They cannot both be true.

The only kind of faith that pleases God is *biblical* faith—which, as we noted on Day 6, is holding what the Bible says to be true. When the writer of Hebrews says that without faith it is impossible to please God (Heb. 11:6), he is referring to biblical faith and no other kind.

The most basic tenet of biblical faith is that God exists, and it is linked to the biblical account of creation because God could only have created the universe if He Himself existed. This is why Hebrews 11:6 concludes by saying, "He who comes to God *must believe that He is*, and that He is a rewarder of those who diligently seek Him." The Greek word *misthapodotes*, meaning rewarder or paymaster, appears only in this verse in the New Testament, and it tells us that God rewards those who earnestly seek Him. *Ekzeteo*, the word translated "diligently seek," emphasizes the outcome intensely desired. Seeking the Lord in this manner includes seeking His *favor*.

God's special blessings are the ways in which He rewards those who diligently seek Him. We cannot expect to receive these blessings if we don't believe that He exists, for we cannot seek someone we think is nonexistent. Both actions—believing that God exists and seeking Him diligently—can only be done through biblical faith.

READ: Matthew 6
REFLECT: Hebrews 11:6
PRAY: Thank the Lord for the gift of biblical faith and pray for someone you know who does not yet possess it.

Day 20
THE KINGDOM

The material universe is God's kingdom because He created it, but Jesus means more than the world of matter when He speaks about the kingdom of God. When He uses the phrase, our Lord is referring to the just and righteous *rule* or *reign* of God. Primarily, this rule is established in individual lives, as individual humans submit themselves to the authority of God and acknowledge Him as their sovereign.

The kingdom of God, a central theme in Scripture, was prophesied in the Old Testament and proclaimed in the New. Psalmists and prophets alike had spoken about it; and it is the subject of the first sermon preached in the New Testament: "Repent, for the kingdom of heaven is at hand" (Matt. 3:2). These words of John the Baptist are quoted verbatim by Jesus when *He* begins preaching (Matt. 4:17).

The Greek word for repentance, *metanoia*, is derived from the verb *metanoeo*, meaning to think differently or reconsider. It implies a change of mind—which of course can only come from a change of *heart*. This is why the call to repentance in Joel 2:13 had said, "Rend your heart and not your garments." Repentance also implies a change of *direction*. We were once walking away from God and the kingdom of heaven, and repentance indicates that we are now walking *towards* them.

We read about the advantages of repentance and the disadvantages of not repenting throughout Scripture. For instance, "He who covers his sins will not prosper, but whoever confesses and forsakes them will have mercy" (Prov. 28:13). The psalmist affirmed that if he had "cherished iniquity" in his heart, the Lord would not have heard his prayer (Ps. 66:18 ESV), but repentance brings God's favor. And in one of the early church's first sermons, Peter urged the people to repent and "turn to God, so that your sins may be wiped out, that times of refreshing shall come from the Lord" (Acts 3:19 NIV).

Jesus' first sermon, "Repent, for the kingdom of heaven is at hand," tells us that we enter the kingdom through the door of repentance. The rest of His teaching makes it clear that living in the kingdom requires a lifestyle of repentance—that is, of daily walking *towards* God rather than away from Him. In His most moving parable, for example, the Prodigal Son leaving the pigsty and returning to his father's house is a picture of repentance.

When Paul testified before King Agrippa, he said that his message to the Jews as well as to the Gentiles was "that they should repent, turn to God, and do works befitting repentance" (Acts 26:20). The works befitting repentance can be summarized as *obedience*. We once had our backs to God and were saying no to Him. Repentance means that we have turned to face Him and are continually saying yes to Him.

READ: Matthew 7
REFLECT: Psalm 32:1
PRAY: Ask God to show you where you have been walking away from Him and receive His grace to turn back to Him.

Day 21
THE KINGDOM'S COMMISSION

Just before His ascension, Jesus commissioned His disciples to expand God's kingdom on earth in these words:

> All authority in heaven and on earth has been given to Me. Therefore go and make disciples of all nations, baptizing them in the name of the Father and of the Son and of the Holy Spirit, and teaching them to obey everything I have commanded you. And surely I am with you always, to the very end of the age. (Matt. 28:18–20)

The thrill of obeying the Great Commission surpasses every other thrill life can offer because of the uniqueness of our leader, our task, our message, and our method.

Our *leader* is the One who has all authority in heaven and earth—the One who gladly paid the ultimate price for us, and at whose name someday every knee will bow (Phil. 2:10). Our *task* is to make disciples of all nations. Anyone who has witnessed even one weak, selfish, guilt-ridden human become transformed into the image of God's Son knows that this is the most rewarding work on earth. Our *message* is love. Not what passes for love in the world, but love as defined and demonstrated by God. And our *method* is faith. Just as the original apostles had to obey Jesus by faith, so too do we.

The Great Commission is as relevant to us today as it was to the early disciples because all nations are not yet Christ's disciples. Our Lord has commissioned us to go and invite them into the kingdom. Our going may or may not involve crossing boundaries of language, culture, or geography, but it invariably involves sharing our faith—both verbally and by how we live our lives. And since every generation has people who are not Christ's disciples, the Great Commission will remain in effect until He returns.

When Abram received Melchizedek's blessing, he was in the period between the promise and its fulfillment. God had already told him that He was going to make him a great nation, but Abram had yet to have even one child. Similarly, we too are living in the "now" and the "not yet" of the kingdom of God.

The kingdom has already been inaugurated by Jesus. On the cross He did all that was required for us to become citizens of heaven, and the outpouring of the Spirit at Pentecost means that we are empowered to be heaven's ambassadors on earth (2 Cor. 5:20). But the kingdom of God will only be *fully* realized when Christ returns—and since no one knows the day or hour, as He said in Matthew 24:36, we must always be ready. This is the sobering moral of the parable of the ten virgins, which immediately follows Jesus' discourse on the end times and which concludes with the warning: "Watch therefore, for you know neither the day nor the hour (Matt. 25:13 ESV).

READ: Matthew 8
REFLECT: Ephesians 5:15–17
PRAY: Ask the Lord to show you one area where you need to obey His last command more fully.

Day 22
THE KINGDOM'S CITIZENS

The Great Commission reveals two key things about the citizens of God's kingdom. First, they belong to *all nations*. Jesus is not content to have *some* nations; He wants them *all!*

Many of the messianic prophecies in the Old Testament specifically mention that all nations are included in God's redemptive plan. For instance, this is what David says in the psalm Jesus quoted from the cross:

> All the ends of the earth Shall remember and turn to the LORD, And all the families of the nations Shall worship before You. For the kingdom is the LORD's, And He rules over the nations. (Ps. 22:27–28)

In the fullness of time, the angel who announced the Savior's birth to the shepherds said, "I bring you good tidings of great joy which will be to *all people*" (Luke 2:10).

Second, the Great Commission tells us that the citizens of God's kingdom are *disciples*. A disciple is one who knows their master's teaching and who obeys it. As Jesus tells His disciples, "If you *know* these things, blessed are you if you *do* them" (John 13:17).

One of the fundamental things disciples know about the kingdom of God is that it is, in Jesus' own words, "not of this world" (John 18:36). And as Paul will later say, "Our citizenship is in heaven" (Phil. 3:20). Consequently, in all areas of life—relational, vocational, financial, or other—Jesus' disciples are to live by the rubrics of heaven.

To live by the rubrics of heaven means that we are led by the Spirit of God and not by the dictates of our flesh, for those who are led by the Spirit are the children of God (Rom. 8:14).

In 1 Corinthians 15:50 Paul categorically says that "flesh and blood cannot inherit the kingdom of God, nor does the perishable inherit the imperishable" (NIV). And in Galatians 5, after enumerating the works of the flesh, he adds, "I warn you, as I warned you before, that those who do such things will not inherit the kingdom of God" (v. 21 ESV). He then lists the nine fruit of the Spirit: "love, joy, peace, patience, kindness, goodness, faithfulness, gentleness, self-control" (vv. 22–23). These are the defining traits of the kingdom's citizens.

As citizens of God's kingdom, our lives must manifest the fruit of the Spirit in increasing measure, and the works of the flesh must be steadily decreasing. As Jesus said, "A good tree does not bear bad fruit, nor does a bad tree bear good fruit" (Luke 6:43). And Peter will remind us that if we abound in qualities like faith, self-control, perseverance, kindness, and love, we will be "neither barren nor unfruitful" in our knowledge of the Lord Jesus Christ (2 Pet. 1:8). At the end of the day, our success as the citizens of God's kingdom depends on *how well we know the King*.

READ: Matthew 9
REFLECT: John 13:17
PRAY: Ask the Lord to show you which fruit of the Spirit you need most and to help you increase in it today.

Day 23

THE KINGDOM'S ADVENTURE

The goal of a first-century disciple was to observe and learn from his teacher to such an extent that he became a virtual replica of the master. "Every one that is perfect shall be as his master," said Jesus in Luke 6:40. He was referring to this idea of the disciple imitating his master to the extent of becoming a replica. He was not saying we can *become* Him. Perhaps as a caution against the false teaching that humans can become divine, Jesus added this preface: "A disciple is not above his master."

When He shared the secrets of the kingdom, our Lord often spoke in parables so that "those on the outside" would not understand (Mark 4:11–12). This is because He is seeking disciples who want to become like Him, not merely inquisitive listeners full of head knowledge. Once inside, the diligent disciple will understand the parables of the kingdom because God's Spirit will give them illumination.

At one point the disciples implore Jesus, "Increase our faith!" In response He replies, "If you have faith as a mustard seed, you can say to this mulberry tree, 'Be pulled up by the roots and be planted in the sea,' and it would obey you" (Luke 17:5–6). This statement teaches us two fundamental things about faith.

The first is that Jesus is not as concerned about the size of our faith as He is about its *quality*. In Matthew 17:20 He has this same seed-sized faith moving a *mountain*, which indicates that He is not even concerned about the size of the obstacle. What He is interested in is *the power that moves obstacles*. The mulberry tree, with its deep, sturdy roots, is not easy to uproot, and Jesus uses it to illustrate what true faith can do. As He says when delivering the boy with the unclean spirit, "All things are possible to him who believes" (Mark 9:23).

The Greek word for possible, *dunatos*, derives from *dunamai*, meaning to be able or to have power. In the Bible *dunatos* speaks of being enabled by God. Thus Jesus' words in Mark 9:23 imply that faith is the God-empowered ability to believe.

The second thing we learn from Jesus' statement in Luke 17:6 is less obvious but equally critical. Just as true faith could potentially change the position of the mulberry tree, true faith changes *our* position. It transplants us from the place of doubt and lack to the place where we can obtain what God has for us. The only way this relocating happens is if we live by faith.

God has given us a great gift in requiring that we live by faith. Living by faith is more than trusting God for our material needs, though it includes that as well. It is maintaining a posture of expectation, a lifestyle of thinking and speaking and behaving as though God is God.

Anyone who truly lives by faith knows that faith makes life an adventure. Faith does not set us up for adventure; *faith is the adventure*.

> READ: Matthew 10
> REFLECT: Mark 9:23
> PRAY: Ask the Holy Spirit to help you become a better disciple of Jesus in one area today.

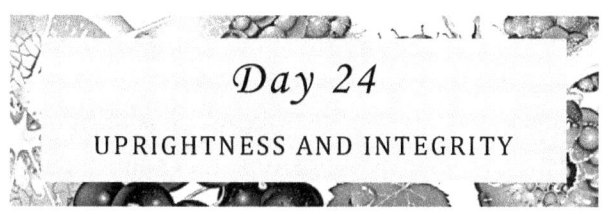

Day 24

UPRIGHTNESS AND INTEGRITY

Zadok, the second name contained in the name Melchizedek, is derived from the word *tsedeq*, meaning righteousness, as noted on Day 19. Of the five men who bear this name in the Old Testament, the most prominent is the first: the priest who descended from Israel's first high priest, Aaron. And like Melchi, Zadok is also in Christ's genealogy: he is the seventh from Jesus (Matt. 1:14). Seven represents wholeness, completeness, and when referring to the character or work of God, *perfection*. Thus the name Zadok, seventh from Jesus' own in the New Testament's opening chapter, is a reminder that our Lord is *perfectly righteous*, and His work on the cross is nothing short of perfection.

These two names in Christ's genealogy, Melchi and Zadok, speak of God's kingdom and His righteousness. If we seek these two things first, Jesus has promised that everything else will fall into place (Matt. 6:33).

We are told throughout Scripture that the righteous will be blessed. The book of Psalms opens with the word blessed, and that is the single best word to describe the righteous life. The Hebrew word *esher* derives from the verb *ashar*, which literally means to be or go straight. Figuratively, it means to be level, right, or happy. The first psalm, which opens with the word blessed, closes with an antithetical statement that contrasts the righteous and the ungodly: "The LORD knows the way of the righteous, But the way of the ungodly shall perish" (v. 6).

Righteous can be defined as *that which is upright*. When the human body is in the upright position, it is standing up straight. In spiritual terms, an upright person is one who is standing up straight *before God*. Uprightness is character that is approved by God, for God is Himself upright (Ps. 92:15).

The Hebrew word for upright, *yashar*, is similar to *ashar*, and it is also used in several senses. Literally, it refers to a thing being vertically erect or horizontally level. In an ethical sense, it means straight and smooth. Like a *yashar* road, the path of the upright is free of those things that would cause them to stumble, and it leads directly to the destination God has for them, with no unnecessary detours. Figuratively, *yashar* also refers to what is agreeable, pleasant, or pleasing. I particularly like this word because it is the root of my name Sharon.

A more contemporary synonym for uprightness, integrity, derives from the Latin *integer*, which represents a whole number. Webster's dictionary defines integrity as the quality or state of being complete or undivided. The Hebrew word for integrity, *tom*, meaning completeness, wholeness, and fullness, is first mentioned in Genesis 20:5. That it is first used by a Gentile, and that God accepts and blesses Abimelech's integrity, indicates His desire for all people to live with integrity. This means that our actions match our words as well as our intentions, and each is blameless in God's sight.

> *READ: Matthew 11*
> *REFLECT: Matthew 6:33*
> *PRAY: Ask the Lord to show you an area where you have not walked with integrity and to help you change.*

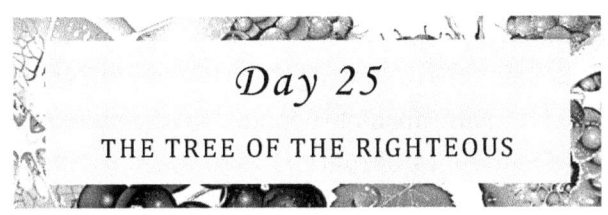

Day 25

THE TREE OF THE RIGHTEOUS

Psalm 92:12 says that the righteous will flourish like a palm tree. The palm is an apt picture of the righteous. It can thrive in hot, arid conditions. Its trunk is straight and strong. Its branches are perennial, and symbolic of victory. And its fruit is nutritious, sweet, and used for oil. To some extent these qualities characterize any upright person, but they are especially true of those who have been made righteous by Christ.

Like the palm, which is among the most upright of trees, the righteous persevere in difficult situations and they maintain integrity even in the smallest, least visible matters. Their lives are consistently marked by fruitfulness and victory. Like the palm's sweet and nutritious fruit, the righteous also have the sweetness of Jesus that attracts others to Him, and they are so filled with God's Word that they can even share its truths with others.

Finally, like the palm tree, the righteous have oil, which represents the anointing of the Holy Spirit. This is obtained from time spent in prayer and worship, and it is a daily infilling. When the psalmist says "I have been anointed with fresh oil" (Ps. 92:10), he is not referring to yesterday's anointing.

The greatest blessing on the righteous comes from the lips of Jesus Himself, in the Sermon on the Mount. The sermon opens with the Beatitudes, a word derived from the Latin *beatitudo*, meaning happiness. This section, Matthew 5:3–10, contains eight parallel statements, each starting with the word blessed and each expressed in the same format: a condition of blessedness followed by the consequence of that blessedness.

One of these conditions is a desire for righteousness so elemental that Jesus describes it as hunger and thirst: "Blessed are those who hunger and thirst for righteousness, for they will be filled" (v. 6).

Not everyone who hungers and thirsts for other things—including life's most basic needs, food and water—is guaranteed fulfillment. People die daily for want of these two necessities. But Jesus has promised that those who hunger and thirst for righteousness *will* be filled.

Jesus's words in Matthew 5:6 echo what was said in Psalm 107:9, that the Lord "satisfies the thirsty and fills the hungry with good things" (NIV). Mary quoted part of this verse in her great hymn of praise after being overshadowed by the Holy Spirit and later receiving Elizabeth's blessing (Luke 1:53). Psalm 107:9 also recalls Psalm 84:11, which has promised, "No good thing will He withhold from those who walk uprightly."

God's blessings are good things, and He will give them to those who live uprightly. Or, to put it in terms of our thesis, to those who are living in a manner that pleases Him.

READ: Matthew 12
REFLECT: Psalm 92:14–15
PRAY: Ask the Lord which quality of the palm tree you need most, and do something to grow in it today.

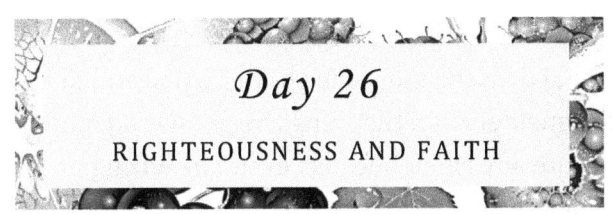

Day 26
RIGHTEOUSNESS AND FAITH

Apart from being an extension of the concept of uprightness, righteousness is the state of being found right. This of course means being found right *by God*.

Only God is perfectly righteous, so His standard of what is right is the only one that counts. Our best righteousness, the best thing we could do on our best day, is like filthy rags (Is. 64:6), and no one enters the presence of a king—an earthly king, let alone the King of the universe—dressed in filthy rags. This is why righteousness has to be given to us *by God*, and we have to receive it *by faith*. This is known as imputed righteousness, and in Romans 4:6 Paul speaks of "the blessedness of the [one] to whom God imputes righteousness apart from works." He then quotes Psalm 32:1–2, to show that imputed righteousness means that our lawless deeds have been *forgiven* and our sins have been *covered*.

The first mention of imputed righteousness appears shortly after Abram has received Melchizedek's blessing, when God visits him in a vision and promises him a son. We are told that in response, Abram "believed in the Lord, and He accounted it to him for righteousness" (Gen. 15:6).

The righteousness Abram is being credited with is not his good deeds but his *faith*. Though he was better than most of us, Abram did do things that were not right, and he would never have been able to stand up straight before God on the basis of his deeds. If he depended on the things he got right, God would also have to take into consideration the things he got *wrong*; and the wrong would negate any right, because even *one* wrong means imperfection when the standard is perfection.

Abraham could only stand up straight or be considered righteous before God because he *believed God's word*. And because his defining trait is that he believed God's word, Abraham has gone down in history as "the man of faith" (Gal. 3:9 NIV), even as the father of all who believe (Rom. 4:11).

Before examining Abraham's faith in Romans 4, Paul says that "no one will be declared righteous in God's sight by the works of the law" (Rom. 3:20 NIV). The phrase "in God's sight" is critical. A person might be considered righteous in others' eyes, and one might even think of themselves as righteous; but it's *God's* eyes that matter, because He is the final judge.

Habakkuk 2:4, which famously says that "the righteous shall live by faith," is quoted three times in the New Testament, in Romans 1:17, Galatians 3:11, and Hebrews 10:38. The word live in this statement encompasses both eternal life, which we receive by faith, as well as how we conduct our lives this side of eternity. It involves how we think, speak, and behave in *this* life. When all of our actions, outward and inward, are done by biblical faith, it is a sure sign that we are righteous.

READ: Matthew 13
REFLECT: Romans 1:17
PRAY: Ask the Lord to help you share at least one part of the gospel with someone today.

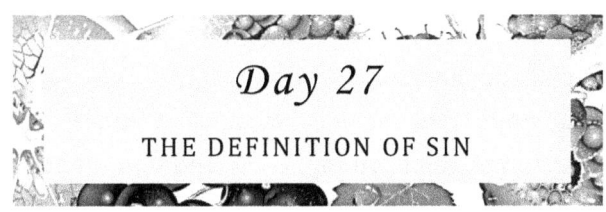

Day 27
THE DEFINITION OF SIN

The first mention of the word righteous refers to Noah—and Noah is called righteous by *God Himself* (Gen. 7:1). In 2 Peter 2:5 he is described as "a preacher of righteousness." Since he lived in an evil and corrupt generation (Gen. 6:5–13), Noah undoubtedly addressed sin when he preached righteousness.

The Bible gives us two simple definitions of sin. First, sin is "lawlessness" (1 John 3:4). Lawlessness involves both *breaking* God's law and *not keeping* it. Thus, sin is doing things that God has told us not to do (sins of commission), and not doing things that God has told us to do (sins of omission). The carnal nature's struggle with these two aspects of sin is memorably described by Paul in Romans 7:19.

Sin or lawlessness is why our Lord had to give His life: He "gave Himself for us, that He might redeem us from every lawless deed" (Titus 2:14). The word translated "lawless deed" is *anomia*, meaning *transgression of the law*. The related adjective *anomos* means *not having or acknowledging the law*.

The Hebrew word for law, *torah*, can also be rendered direction, instruction(s), and teaching(s). It is derived from the verb *yarah*, meaning to throw (lots) or shoot (arrows). The archery term evokes the sense of pointing with a finger and thus, of instructing or directing towards the mark. This depicts sin as "missing the mark." The Greek word for sin, *hamartia*, also means a failure to hit the mark.

At the obvious level, the mark we miss when we sin is the *torah*—the teachings, instructions, laws, and commands that God has given us. This is the level of behavior, and behavior includes our thoughts, words, and deeds. But at a deeper, more visceral level, the level of our inner being or nature, the mark we miss when we sin is *the glory of God*: as Romans 3:23 says, "All have sinned and fall short of the glory of God."

We miss the mark in our behavior because, since the first act of human sin, we have missed the mark in our nature. *We sin because we are sinful.* Children don't have to be taught to choose wrong, for it comes naturally; they have to be taught to choose *right*. This is why Isaiah says, "When Your judgments are in the earth, The inhabitants of the world *learn* righteousness" (Is. 26:9).

The Bible's second definition of sin is that sin is "all unrighteousness" (1 John 5:17). Thus, *anything* that cannot be defined as righteousness is sin.

Defining sin as "all unrighteousness" helps us to accurately classify those areas of commission and omission about which the Bible is silent. It gives us a yardstick: if a particular act qualifies as unrighteousness, it's sin. When an act falls in the "grey areas" of morality, the Holy Spirit alone can tell us whether it is unrighteous, for one of His roles is to "convict the world concerning sin and righteousness" (John 16:8 NASB).

> *READ: Matthew 14*
> *REFLECT: Titus 2:14*
> *PRAY: Thank the Lord for redeeming you from sin, and commit yourself to greater righteousness today.*

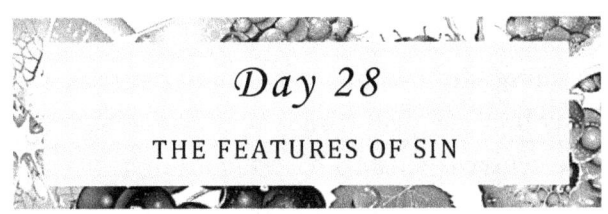

Day 28

THE FEATURES OF SIN

The Bible's first mention of sin appears in Genesis 4:7. The context is Cain's jealousy of Abel, when God comes to Cain with a word of warning: "If you do not do what is right, sin is crouching at your door; it desires to have you, but you must rule over it" (NIV). God's words to Cain reveal four critical features of sin.

First, sin is associated with not "doing well." This is the literal translation of the verb *yatab* in Genesis 4:7. The sense it conveys is of one's inner state rather than merely outward behavior. The connection between Cain's internal condition and the act he eventually committed was a close one, because the act originated in his heart. This is why Solomon advises, "Above all else, guard your heart, for everything you do flows from it" (Prov. 4:23 NIV).

Second, when we are not doing well internally, sin is not far off. It is in fact right at our door, crouching in wait as a predator for its prey. And since we know from Genesis 4:7 that sin is what's outside when we are not "doing well," we must be especially careful not to open the door at such times. As Paul has advised, "Be angry and do not sin; . . . and *give no opportunity to the devil*" (Eph. 4:26–27 ESV).

Third, just as a predator desires to overpower its prey, so also sin wants to master us. It wants to "have dominion" over us, to use Paul's term in Romans 6:14. Many Christians glibly quote the second clause of this verse—"You are not under law but under grace"—because they are helpless in their battle against sin and the only way they can deal with it is by sweeping it under a rug called grace, *whereas the only covering for sin is the sinless blood of our Lord Jesus*. Grace is not the covering for sin but the power by which we receive both the atonement Jesus made for us, as well as the ability to daily live sanctified lives.

The theme of Romans 6, death to sin, suggests that the point of verse 14 is found in its *first* clause: "Sin shall not have dominion over you." Our not being under law but under grace is evidenced by *Jesus* having dominion over us. Otherwise we remain in a perpetual cycle of sin, guilt, and forgiveness, with no dominion to speak of.

Finally, Genesis 4:7 tells us how God wants us to respond to sin: He wants us to rule over it. Victory over sin is *always* God's desire for us.

Cain shows a cavalier disregard for the word of the Lord and refuses to heed its warning. He is the archetype of those who live by the dictates of their flesh and not by the Spirit. His murder of Abel is a sobering reminder that Adam's nature got passed down to the human race. That nature, in a nutshell, is the desire to gratify what the flesh craves rather than to fulfill the will of God. This is why Paul urges, "Walk by the Spirit and you will not gratify the desires of the flesh" (Gal. 5:16 NIV).

READ: Matthew 15
REFLECT: Galatians 5:16
PRAY: Ask the Lord to help you walk by the Spirit in any area of weakness you may encounter today.

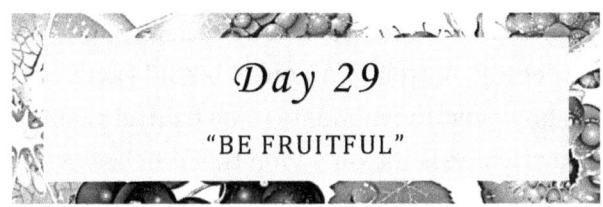

Day 29
"BE FRUITFUL"

When the Pharisees ask Jesus if divorce is lawful, He begins, as He often does, by posing a counter-question. On this occasion He asks, "What did Moses command you?" (Mark 10:3). Jesus knows what Moses commanded, but He is going to show them that their starting point is incorrect. The starting point of the debate is not divorce but *marriage*, because that came first, and so Jesus directs the conversation to Creation.

Our discussion on righteousness has brought us to the law, and we too must start at the real starting point. Rather than beginning with what God commanded Moses, we must first look at what He commanded *Adam*. Long before the Ten Commandments, there were the Two Commandments—and these were also a "Thou shalt" and a "Thou shalt not."

The first Creation Commandment, given immediately after God created and blessed humankind, was this:

> *Be fruitful* and multiply; fill the earth and subdue it; *have dominion* over the fish of the sea, over the birds of the air, and over every living thing that moves on the earth. (Gen. 1:28)

God's first recorded words to human beings, "Be fruitful," tell us that *fruitfulness is our God-ordained destiny*. Being fruitful is more than biological reproduction. It is about being *productive*.

God wants each person to lead a productive and purposeful life, and to "enjoy oneself in all one's labor" (Eccl. 5:18 NASB). Ultimately, however, the mandate to be fruitful is about bearing *spiritual* fruit, which is the only kind that will last. As Jesus Himself has said, "I chose you and appointed you to go and bear fruit—fruit that will *last*" (John 15:16 NIV).

Spiritual fruitfulness represents what God does *in* us as well as *through* us, and it is the best evidence of spiritual maturity. Just as a cherry sapling cannot bear cherries until it becomes a tree, so also we cannot bear "fruit that will last" if we remain spiritual saplings. A cherry seedling planted in a commercial orchard is expected to grow into a tree and bear cherries at the proper time. If it never produces anything, or stops producing, it gets cut down. This is what our Lord is driving at in John 15:6, when He says that anyone who does not abide in Him is "cast out as a [withered] branch."

Spiritual maturity and fruitfulness come as we keep His commandments and thereby abide in His love: as Jesus goes on to say, "If you keep My commandments, you will abide in My love" (John 15:10). When we abide or live in His love, we will produce spiritual fruit, and that is the fruit we should be seeking if we want our lives to count for eternity. Every other kind of fruit, however wholesome and good, will not last beyond this life.

READ: Matthew 16
REFLECT: John 15:16
PRAY: Ask God to show you some of the fruit He wants you to bear and to help you abide in His love today.

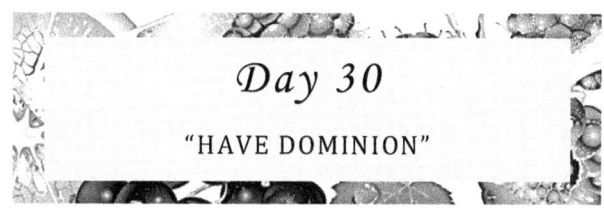

Day 30

"HAVE DOMINION"

The next part of the first Creation Commandment, "have dominion," is not limited to politics, government, and law enforcement. Instead, it refers to *gaining mastery*. We fulfill this mandate when we acquire a new skill—*any* new skill. Even a baby is displaying dominion when she learns to say "Mama" or hold the bottle by herself.

One of the greatest manifestations of having dominion is when we acquire mastery over *ourselves*, and nowhere is this more apparent than in our areas of weakness. Time was we could never say no to chocolate or yes to exercising, but with enough effort and practice we mastered these areas of weakness. Or perhaps we used to struggle with self-pity, and then we read the right motivational book, applied the principles, and soon found ourselves feeling optimistic and cheerful.

Weaknesses like these anyone can master, whether the Holy Spirit indwells them or not, because the mandate to have dominion was given to all. If one has enough determination and is willing to put in the necessary effort, anyone can eat better, exercise more, or—other things being equal—climb Mount Everest.

But there exists a whole realm that we cannot master without the help of the Holy Spirit, and this is the realm ruled by our flesh. The flesh is hostile to God (Rom. 8:7) and at war with the Spirit

(Gal. 5:17), and it can only be overcome by the grace of God: as Paul affirms,

> For the grace of God has appeared that offers salvation to all people. It teaches us to say "No" to ungodliness and worldly passions, and to live self-controlled, upright and godly lives in the present age. (Titus 2:11–12 NIV)

Mastering our flesh requires that we *subjugate* it. When Paul says "I discipline my body and bring it into subjection" (1 Cor. 9: 27), the second verb used, *doulagogeo*, literally means *to treat as a slave*. If we don't want our flesh to have dominion over us, we must treat it as a slave, for "people are slaves to whatever has mastered them" (2 Pet. 2:19 NIV). Obedience is key in this process, for we are "slaves of the one [we] obey" (Rom. 6:16 NIV).

Enduring trials is another aspect of having dominion. Trials must mature us and make us more submitted to God, or we have suffered in vain. God loves and wants to bless us all, but we must prove that we will handle His special blessings in a mature, responsible manner, and only trials refine our character to that extent. Throughout the New Testament we are urged to persevere, endure, and even "count it all joy" (James 1:2) when we encounter trials.

Storms are an inescapable part of nature, and if a cherry sapling wants to fulfill its destiny of becoming a tree that bears cherries, it must emerge stronger and not weaker after a storm.

READ: Matthew 17
REFLECT: James 1:2–3
PRAY: Thank the Lord for a trial you have faced, and pray for someone you know who is going through a trial.

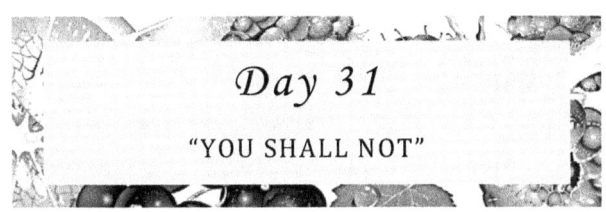

Day 31
"YOU SHALL NOT"

The second Creation Commandment qualifies as a "Thou shalt not" because the Lord is forbidding something:

> Of every tree of the garden you may freely eat; but of the tree of the knowledge of good and evil *you shall not* eat, for in the day that you eat of it you shall surely die. (Gen. 2:16–17)

It is important to note that the command does not begin with what is prohibited but with what is *permitted*. God wants Adam to know what he can enjoy before he is told what he cannot enjoy; and the fact that *every other tree* was available reflects God's generosity.

The trees in Eden represent the three primary branches of knowledge: *natural*, *moral*, and *spiritual*. Those from which Adam may freely eat represent knowledge of the natural world. The tree of the knowledge of good and evil represents moral knowledge. And the tree of life represents spiritual knowledge.

Fulfilling God's first Creation Commandment to be fruitful and have dominion over the earth required knowledge of the natural world, and God gave Adam free access to this. In fact, He even allowed him to *invent* such knowledge by letting him name the animals (Gen. 2:19). Natural knowledge is granted to this day: as the psalmist says, "The earth He has given to the children of men" (Ps. 115:16).

We can use our knowledge of the natural world for good or for evil in any sphere of human industry, and this comes from our having been created with free will. We are capable of making both wrong choices and right because we're endowed with the gift of free will.

Spiritual knowledge, represented by the tree of life, can be summed up as the knowledge of God and eternal life. "This is eternal life," Jesus said in the High Priestly prayer, *"that they may know You"* (John 17:3). Adam had this knowledge in his prelapsarian state, even without eating of the tree of life, because he enjoyed unbroken communion with God and he had not yet died spiritually. The tree of life became protected only after the Fall (Gen. 3:24). This is proof of God's mercy, for if Adam and Eve had eaten of it in their fallen state, they would have lived forever *in that state*, and that would rule out the possibility of redemption.

The tree of life is of course a shadow of the cross, which the apostles sometimes refer to as "the tree." For instance, Peter tells the council in Jerusalem, "The God of our fathers raised up Jesus whom you murdered by hanging on a tree" (Acts 5:30). Later, when writing to the church, he says Jesus "bore our sins in His own body on the tree, that we, having died to sins, might live for righteousness" (1 Pet. 2:24).

READ: Matthew 18
REFLECT: 1 Peter 2:24
PRAY: Thank Jesus for enduring the cross for you and ask Him to help you walk worthy of that sacrifice today.

Day 32

GOOD AND EVIL

The tree that was forbidden in Eden is the one that represents moral knowledge. To understand why moral knowledge was off-limits, we need to realize that the term "the knowledge of good and evil" is a *merism*, a figure of speech that uses pairs of antonyms to denote an entirety. "Good" and "evil" cover the spectrum of moral knowledge, and God wanted Adam to stay away from it for a very good reason: he was not God.

God is the only one who can see the entire moral spectrum, and as the King and supreme Judge of the universe He alone can determine what is good and what is evil. By disobeying God Adam was declaring independence. He was saying that he would set his own rules about right and wrong and so be his own god. This is the essence of the Adamic nature we have all inherited from our first father.

Eden before the Fall was undefiled. At Creation God had declared everything good, but the entrance of sin meant that good must now coexist with evil. Therefore, when pondering the existence of evil, we must also take into account the existence of *good*, because the world that our first parents left us is not the one they received.

Given that we inhabit a world where good and evil dwell alongside, we are exhorted to be "wise about what is good, and innocent about what is evil" (Rom. 16:19 NIV). Innocence is not to be confused with immaturity: as the writer of Hebrews observes,

> Everyone who partakes only of milk is unskilled in the word of righteousness, for he is a babe. But solid food belongs to those who are of full age, that is, those who by reason of use have their senses exercised to discern both good and evil. (Heb. 5:13–14)

Spiritual maturity is discerning what is good and what is evil, which means *distinguishing between them and choosing the good*. This constitutes wisdom, and "Blessed are those who find wisdom" (Prov. 3:13). Conversely, "Woe to those who call evil good, and good evil" (Is. 5:20).

Genesis 2:17 contains the first instance of the word die. God warned Adam upfront that eating of the forbidden tree would result in death, but God does not want anyone to die: "As surely as I live, declares the Sovereign Lord, I take no pleasure in the death of the wicked, but rather that they turn from their ways and live" (Ezek. 33:11 NIV). And Peter tells us that the Lord is "patient with you, not wanting anyone to perish, but everyone to come to repentance" (2 Pet. 3:9 NIV).

Not only does God not want anyone to die, but He is also not the author of death. Death is merely the consequence of sin. As Romans 6:23 puts it, the wages of sin is death.

READ: Matthew 19
REFLECT: Hebrews 5:13–14
PRAY: Ask the Lord to help you discern good from evil in one area today.

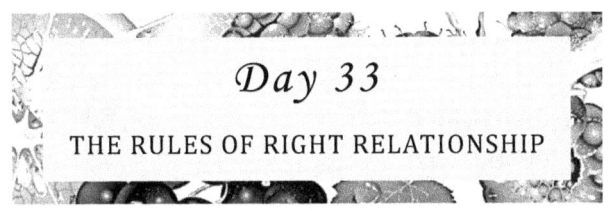

Day 33

THE RULES OF RIGHT RELATIONSHIP

Just as a person needs to learn the traffic laws in order to obtain a driver's license, the Israelites needed to know the rudiments of being God's covenant people before they could enter the Promised Land. But before He gave them these rudimentary rules in Exodus 20, the Lord made what is known as the Mosaic covenant in Exodus 19. We can infer from the sequence—the covenant *preceding* the law—that God places His covenant above man's ability to keep the law.

The Israelites had just emerged from four centuries of slavery. Like an inexperienced driver, they needed to be taught the basics of behaving and relating as God's people. The Ten Commandments address behavior, but even more fundamentally, they address *relationship*. In other words, the law is about *maintaining* relationship, not *attaining* it.

The law is not a means of salvation. If it were, then salvation would depend on our ability to keep it, or our works, and God had a more reliable plan: the perfect work of His perfect Son. We are saved by grace through faith, so that no one can boast (Eph. 2:8–9). The law does not save. It merely teaches us how to relate in a manner that pleases God, and obeying it incurs the blessings God has promised for obedience.

Obedience is also an *evidence* of faith: when we obey God we are saying that we take Him at His word, and that is faith. Even Abraham demonstrated his faith by obedience, for "his faith was made complete by what he did" (James 2:22 NIV).

The only connection the law has with salvation is that it reveals our inability to save ourselves. The law reveals our sin—"through the law we become conscious of our sin" (Rom. 3:20 NIV)—and our sin reveals our need for a savior. Thus it points us to Jesus: as Paul says, "The law was our schoolmaster to bring us unto Christ, that we might be justified by faith" (Gal. 3:24 KJV).

Relationship with God on the basis of His grace is the starting point of our citizenship in His kingdom. That is why when Jesus tells Nicodemus how a person enters the kingdom, He says, "Unless one *is born again*, he cannot see the kingdom of God" (John 3:3). He does not say, "Unless one *keeps the law*, he cannot see the kingdom of God."

As a Pharisee Nicodemus would have been extremely familiar with the Mosaic law, for the Pharisees were zealous for the law. In John 3:1 Nicodemus is described as "a ruler of the Jews," which indicates that he was a member of the Sanhedrin, the Jewish ruling council. He knew all the rules, far beyond the Ten Commandments. And it is to this person, well-versed in the law and punctilious about observing it, that Jesus makes His most famous statement: "For God so loved the world that He gave His only begotten Son, that whoever believes in Him should not perish but have everlasting life" (John 3:16).

> READ: Matthew 20
> REFLECT: James 2:26
> PRAY: Ask the Lord to show you the commandment you need to obey most, and obey Him today.

Day 34
GREATER RIGHTEOUSNESS

In the Sermon on the Mount Jesus says something that would have been radical for His original audience. He says, "Unless your righteousness exceeds that of the scribes and Pharisees, you will never enter the kingdom of heaven" (Matt. 5:20).

This was radical because the people considered the scribes and Pharisees to be guaranteed admission into the kingdom of heaven because of their superior righteousness. But Jesus is saying that a person's righteousness should surpass the virtue outwardly displayed by the scribes and Pharisees. It must go past the outward to the inward, past words and actions to the motives and attitudes of the heart. And this is what this greater righteousness looks like: being enraged with someone is equal to murder, and looking at a woman with lust is equal to adultery (Matt. 5:22,28).

Since it is easier to be angry and feel lust than it is to commit murder or adultery, the righteousness Jesus is describing exceeds that of the scribes and Pharisees because *they* were guilty of anger and lust as well! While they could not be faulted in the external matters of murder, adultery, theft, and lies, they were guilty of the internal equivalents: anger, lust, covetousness, and hypocrisy. That is why in the instance of the woman caught in adultery, when Jesus says that whoever is without sin can cast the first stone, one by one the scribes and Pharisees all leave, "being convicted by their conscience" (John 8:9).

After setting this radical new standard of righteousness, Jesus proceeds to demand *an even higher* standard:

> You have heard that it was said, "An eye for an eye and a tooth for a tooth." *But I say to you*, Do not resist the one who is evil. But if anyone slaps you on the right cheek, turn to him the other also.... You have heard that it was said, "You shall love your neighbor and hate your enemy." *But I say to you*, Love your enemies and pray for those who persecute you, so that you may be sons of your Father who is in heaven. (Matt. 5:38–39,43–45 ESV)

To be like our Father in heaven, we must not only not repay evil with evil, *but we must also repay evil with good*. When someone wrongs us, it is not enough to not take revenge. We are to also love, bless, and pray for them! To drive home the point, Jesus goes on to ask a series of rhetorical questions:

> If you love those who love you, what reward do you have? Do not even the tax collectors do the same? And if you greet only your brothers, what more are you doing than others? Do not even the Gentiles do the same? (Matt. 5:46–47 ESV)

Our Lord has set us a very high standard of righteousness, keeping which is impossible without His enabling grace. And it is possible only when we understand that *it's all about love*.

READ: Matthew 21
REFLECT: Matthew 5:44–45
PRAY: Think of someone who has hurt you and ask the Lord to help you forgive them.

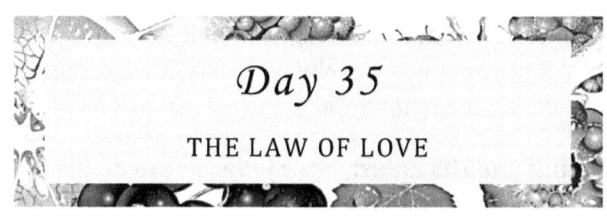

Day 35
THE LAW OF LOVE

When an expert in the law asks Jesus to name the greatest commandment, Jesus sums up the law in the word love:

> "You shall love the LORD your God with all your heart, with all your soul, and with all your mind." This is the first and great commandment. And the second is like it: "You shall love your neighbor as yourself." On these two commandments hang all the Law and the Prophets. (Matt. 22:37–40)

As Paul will later say, "Love is the fulfillment of the law" (Rom. 13:10).

From His first discourse to the last, Jesus consistently taught the same message about love. Towards the end of the Sermon on the Mount, He summarizes His teaching by saying, "So in everything, do to others what you would have them do to you, for this sums up the Law and the Prophets" (Matt. 7:12 NIV). This is the golden rule, the one rule that should govern all our behavior and relationships, as "in everything" implies.

In 1 Corinthians 13 Paul gives us a definition of love that is more accurately a *description* of love. In telling us what love is, the apostle tells us what love *does*. And this what love does:

> Love is patient, love is kind. It does not envy, it does not boast, it is not proud. It does not dishonor others, it is not self-seeking, it is not easily angered, it keeps no record of

wrongs. Love does not delight in evil but rejoices with the truth. It always protects, always trusts, always hopes, always perseveres. Love never fails. (1 Cor. 13:4–8 NIV)

On the night of His arrest, after Judas left to do his worst deed, Jesus told the remaining eleven,

> A new commandment I give to you, that you love one another; as I have loved you, that you also love one another. By this all will know that you are My disciples, if you have love for one another. (John 13:34–35)

Within moments of giving this commandment, Jesus began the final excruciating journey to the cross, to demonstrate the full measure of God's love for the world. The events of the next day so transformed the eleven that they became wholehearted lovers like their Lord.

Obedience to the new commandment can only be achieved by the Spirit, not through any fleshly effort, for "the flesh profits nothing" (John 6:63). If we attempt it by trusting in our own abilities, the result will be self-righteousness. Self-righteousness is unrighteousness and therefore the opposite of love.

Love is true righteousness. It is the defining rule of the kingdom of God, and thus it is our badge of identity as citizens of the kingdom.

READ: Matthew 22
REFLECT: 1 Corinthians 13:4
PRAY: Ask God which quality in 1 Corinthians 13:4–8 you need most, and to help you grow in it today.

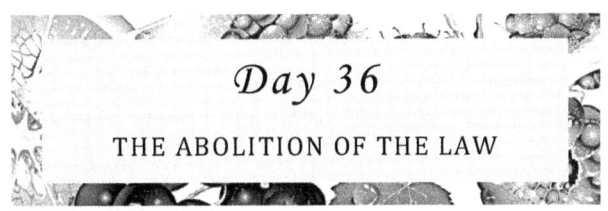

Day 36
THE ABOLITION OF THE LAW

At various points in His ministry, Jesus rebuked the scribes and Pharisees because they were only concerned with outward righteousness, but He never advocated that they do away with the law. On the contrary, He reprimanded them for *transgressing* the commandment of God for the sake of their traditions (Matt. 15:3). And in the Sermon on the Mount He plainly stated that He had "not come to abolish the Law and the Prophets but to fulfill them" (Matt. 5:17 ESV).

Many take "fulfill" to mean that Jesus fulfilled the law by keeping it perfectly and by His atoning death on our behalf. While this is true, Matthew 5:17 is only the opening part of a statement that continues in the next two verses:

> For truly, I say to you, *until heaven and earth pass away*, not an iota, not a dot, will pass from the Law until all is accomplished. Therefore whoever ... does [these commandments] and teaches them will be called great in the kingdom. (Matt. 5:18–19 ESV)

Jesus indeed kept the law perfectly and fulfilled all that was required for our salvation. But since heaven and earth have not yet passed away, according to our Lord the law is still in effect—not as a means of salvation but as a guide to right living, as we saw on Day 33.

The abolition of the law has been the steady, systematic work of the devil, and he has done it from *within* the church, by a heresy known as antinomianism, which purports to liberate people from condemnation by declaring that the law has been abolished. The word sin itself is steadily being expunged from our vocabulary, even in the church, and someday it may be banned altogether. Things are being set in place for the arrival of the antichrist, whom Paul calls "the man of lawlessness" (2 Thess. 2:3 NIV).

The devil's intention to abolish the law is evident when we recall the first thing he said to human beings: "Has God indeed said 'You shall not . . . ?'" (Gen. 3:1).

Many have noted that the serpent caused Eve to doubt God's word, but it is equally important to note that the specific word he attacked was *God's commandment.* And he has been deceiving humankind about God's commandments ever since. He tempts us to either disobey what the law says or to disbelieve its existence, so that when the "man of lawlessness" appears the world will not recognize or oppose him.

The Bible's final book tells us that the end-time people of God will be those "who keep his commands and remain faithful to Jesus" (Rev. 14:12 NIV). From this we can infer that the apostate church will consist of those who fall away, both from the commands of God and from His Son.

READ: Matthew 23
REFLECT: Revelation 14:12
PRAY: Ask the Lord to show you which area you need to be more faithful, and do something about it today.

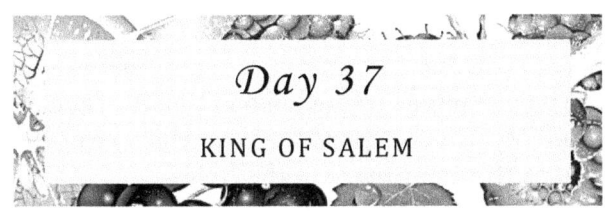

Day 37
KING OF SALEM

Not only does Melchizedek's name mean king of righteousness, but he actually *is* a king. He is king of Salem, we learn from Genesis 14:18, which also tells us that he is the priest of God Most High. These two functions of king and priest are critical to understanding Melchizedek as a type of Christ.

Salem means peace, and as king of a city named peace, Melchizedek is the perfect person to offer Abram a benediction of peace as he is emerging from war. Salem is the original name of Jerusalem, which means *possession of peace*.

Jerusalem is first mentioned in Joshua 10, which records Israel's campaign in southern Canaan on the day the sun stood still. The opening verse contains a reference to Adonizedek king of Jerusalem. A compound of Adonai and *tsedeq*, Adonizedek means *lord of righteousness*. The similarity between his name and Melchizedek's is obvious, but the bearers of the names are diametrically opposite in their treatment of Abram and his descendants: whereas Melchizedek blesses Abram, Adonizedek will attack the Israelites.

After Joshua's death the children of Judah fight against Jerusalem and take the city (Judg. 1:8). This is fitting, given that Judah is Jesus' ancestor and Jerusalem is His possession. As Zechariah will later prophesy,

> Sing and rejoice, O daughter of Zion! For behold, I am coming and I will dwell in your midst, says the LORD. Many nations will be joined to the LORD in that day, and they shall become My people.... And the LORD will take possession of Judah as His inheritance in the Holy Land, and will again choose Jerusalem. (Zech. 2:10–12)

Another of Zechariah's prophecies concerning Jerusalem foretells one of the most momentous events in Jesus' earthly ministry, the triumphal entry. Writing by divine inspiration centuries beforehand, the prophet had said:

> Rejoice greatly, O daughter of Zion! Shout, O daughter of Jerusalem! Behold, your King is coming to you; He is just and having salvation, Lowly and riding on a donkey, A colt, the foal of a donkey. (Zech. 9:9)

As we know from the Gospels, Jesus entered Jerusalem riding on a donkey just days before He was crucified. On that first Palm Sunday, the residents of Jerusalem had welcomed Him into their city with cries of "Hosanna to the Son of David! Blessed is He who comes in the name of the LORD!" (Matt. 21:9). They were quoting from Psalm 118, which was a thanksgiving liturgy accompanying the procession of a king into the Temple precincts. What the people of Jerusalem spoke over Jesus is what the priests would have said as they blessed the king.

READ: Matthew 24
REFLECT: Psalm 118:28–29
PRAY: Pray that Jerusalem's residents will realize that Jesus is the promised Messiah and will worship Him.

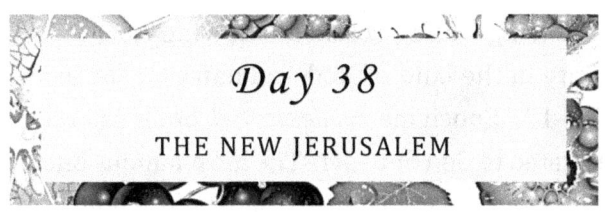

Day 38
THE NEW JERUSALEM

Melchizedek's association with Salem, whatever it was historically, is extremely meaningful typologically, for Melchizedek is a type of Christ, and our Lord has an eternal relationship with Jerusalem. Not only was He condemned and crucified in the city, but He will also return to rule from there. The New Jerusalem, as we are told in the Bible's penultimate chapter, descends to earth from heaven:

> I saw the Holy City, the new Jerusalem, coming down out of heaven from God, prepared as a bride beautifully dressed for her husband. And I heard a loud voice from the throne saying, "Look! God's dwelling place is now among the people, and he will dwell with them." (Rev. 21:2–3 NIV)

John's vision recalls the final words of Ezekiel. Hundreds of years previously the prophet had declared that Jerusalem's new name would be "THE LORD IS THERE" (Ezek. 48:35).

The book of Revelation also shows us an evil city, Babylon, described as a whore and thus contrasted with the New Jerusalem, which is a *bride*. As we saw on Day 10, Babylon is the new name of Babel, the site of the doomed tower. The New Jerusalem is also antithetical to the first city mentioned in the Bible—the city that Cain built.

After leaving God's presence following Abel's murder, Cain builds a city in the land of Nod and names it for his son Enoch (Gen. 4:16–17). Enoch means *dedicated*, but it can refer to something dedicated to God or to evil. The most famous Enoch, seventh from Adam from the godly line of Seth, was wholly dedicated to God, and he is the first man said to have "walked with God" and been translated to heaven without experiencing death (Gen. 5:24).

The Bible's concluding chapter tells us that entrance to the New Jerusalem is barred to people who do not repent: "Outside are the dogs, those who practice magic arts, the sexually immoral, the murderers, the idolaters and whoever loves and practices falsehood" (Rev. 22:15 NIV). This list of sins, the last of its kind in Scripture, is an unambiguous one, and this verse also contains the final mention of love. *Phileo*, the Greek verb used, means to show warm affection in intimate friendship. It is sobering that the last time this word appears, it is in association with *falsehood*.

After Adam and Eve were banished from Eden, God installed cherubim at the garden, "and a flaming sword which turned every way, to guard the way to the tree of life" (Gen. 3:25). But because Jesus regained paradise, those who trust in Him will have access to the tree of life: as Revelation 22:14 promises, "Blessed are those who do His commandments, that they may have the right to the tree of life, and may enter through the gates to the city."

READ: Matthew 25
REFLECT: Revelation 22:14
PRAY: Pray for someone you know who is not living in a manner that pleases the Lord.

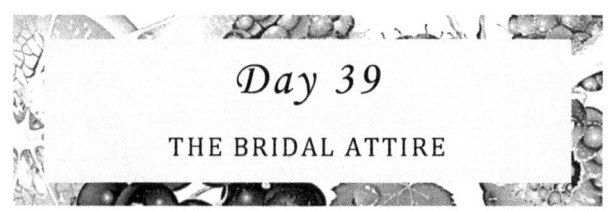

Day 39

THE BRIDAL ATTIRE

John's vision of the New Jerusalem as a bride harks back to the opening chapters of the Bible, because at the dawn of human history there was a bride. According to rabbinic tradition, Eve was adorned with a glorious raiment when God presented her to Adam, and thus the first bridal dress foreshadows the last. Even before John saw the New Jerusalem descending from heaven, he had heard a great multitude shouting,

> Hallelujah! For our Lord God Almighty reigns. Let us rejoice and be glad and give him glory! For the wedding of the Lamb has come, and his bride has made herself ready. Fine linen, bright and clean, was given her to wear. (Fine linen stands for the righteous acts of God's holy people.) (Rev. 19:6–8 NIV)

Revelation 19:8 contains one of the great paradoxes that lie at the heart of our faith: fine linen is *given* to the bride, yet it also refers to the righteous acts *of God's holy people*. We find a similar paradox in Ephesians 2:8–10, which says we are saved through faith, *not by works*, and that we are God's workmanship, "created in Christ Jesus *for good works*" (v. 10). How can it be both?

The answer is found in the term "His workmanship" (and "His bride" in Revelation 19:7). The possessives imply that it's all about being *related to God*. If we are related to God through His Son, then our good works count. Otherwise, they are tattered and filthy rags, unable to cover our nakedness, far less to *adorn* us. They are wholly different from what God clothes us with, the glorious attire that Isaiah has described in these words:

> My soul will exult in my God, for He has clothed me with *garments of salvation*, He has wrapped me with *a robe of righteousness*, as a bridegroom decks himself with a garland, and a bride adorns herself with jewels. (Is. 61:10 NASB)

This metaphor of clothing also appears in the New Testament epistles. Paul instructs us to clothe ourselves with the armor of light and with Christ (Rom. 13:12,14); to put on the new self (Eph. 4:24); and to wear compassion, kindness, humility, gentleness, patience, and above all love (Col. 3:12,14). Peter uses the metaphor as well. "Be clothed with humility," he says in 1 Peter 5:5. And knowing how much women like clothes, he tells them:

> Do not let your adornment be merely outward—arranging the hair, wearing gold, or putting on fine apparel—rather let it be the hidden person of the heart, with the incorruptible beauty of a gentle and quiet spirit, which is very precious in the sight of God. (1 Pet. 3:3–4)

READ: Matthew 26
REFLECT: Colossians 3:12–14
PRAY: Ask the Lord which part of the "bridal attire" you need to wear better, and wear it better today.

Day 40

THE PRINCE OF PEACE

The title "king of Salem" appears twice in Hebrews 7, where the priesthood of Jesus is likened to Melchizedek's. The writer even adds "meaning 'king of peace'" after the second instance (v. 2), to draw our attention to the prophecy in Isaiah 9, where the Messiah was called Sar Shalom, the Prince of Peace.

The Jewish concept of *shalom* implies more than the absence of unpleasant things like war, conflict, or turmoil. It also includes the presence of desirable things like completeness, soundness, prosperity, and welfare. This makes it similar to the Hebrew concept of blessing. Other meanings of the word encompass physical safety and soundness, tranquility and contentment, and friendship and friendliness. In their fullest form, these levels of peace can only come from the Prince of Peace.

In Ephesians 2:14–17 Paul tells us that Jesus is our peace, He has made our peace, and He has preached peace to us. Peace is thus His *nature*, His *work*, and His *message*. The peace that our Lord gives is far-reaching, covering every dimension in which peace is needed—upward, inward, and outward.

The peace we have with God is ours because Jesus reconciled all things to God "by making peace through his blood, shed on the cross" (Col. 1:20 NIV). We were once God's enemies, but Christ's sacrificial death signed the peace treaty, for "the punishment that brought us peace was on him" (Is. 53:5 NIV). As Paul affirms, "Having been justified by faith, we have peace with God through our Lord Jesus" (Rom. 5:1).

The first of the many references to Jesus' priesthood in Hebrews relates to His making peace with God on our behalf:

> In all things He had to be made like His brethren, that He might be a merciful and faithful High Priest in things pertaining to God, to make propitiation for the sins of the people. (Heb. 2:17)

The verb translated "make propitiation," *hilaskomai*, refers to the act of showing mercy by conciliating God's wrath. It appears only here and in Luke 18:13, where the penitent tax collector in Jesus' parable prays a simple but heartfelt prayer that God will answer: "God, *be merciful* to me a sinner!"

God's wrath is not a capricious or unbridled outburst of anger. It is His consistent and righteous response to sin. If He tolerated sin, it would violate His holiness. If He let it go unpunished, it would violate His justice. And if He did not provide a solution, it would violate His mercy. At the cross God's holiness, justice, and mercy meet in perfect harmony.

Peace with God means that we need no longer fear the wrath to come (Rom. 5:9; 1 Thess. 1:10). Jesus Himself assured us that whoever hears His word and believes in the Father "shall not come into judgment but has passed from death to life" (John 5:24). Our *work* will be judged (2 Cor. 5:10), but *we* won't be sentenced to death.

READ: Matthew 27

REFLECT: Ephesians 2:14–17

PRAY: Thank Jesus for making peace between you and God, and pray for someone who does not yet have this peace.

Day 41

INWARD PEACE

Internal peace, the peace within our hearts, also comes from the One who promised to give us rest for our souls (Matt. 11:29).

There are many ways of becoming calmer apart from Jesus—shopping sprees, massages, and medications, to name a few—but these are temporary palliatives, relaxing us for a spell and then wearing off. And when the effect wears off, the pain we experience is usually more acute. This means we will need an even stronger dose next time.

Furthermore, even if we may feel at peace in the present moment, does anyone know what they will face tomorrow? No matter how carefully we may plan for the future, we have not actually *lived* it yet. A peace that is not "here today and gone tomorrow" comes from the One who is "the same yesterday, today, and forever" (Heb. 13:8). And He has said,

> Peace I leave with you; my peace I give to you. Not as the world gives do I give to you. Let not your hearts be troubled, neither let them be afraid. (John 14:27 ESV)

Jesus has already left us His peace. Our part is to receive it and to *let not* our heart be troubled. The word let indicates that we have a choice to make—and only we can make that choice for ourselves. Similarly, only we can do what Paul advises in Colossians 3:15, "*Let* the peace of Christ rule in your hearts" (ESV).

This inward peace is necessary not just in the face of fear and anxiety but also when we encounter guilt and shame. We usually tend to seek quick relief from guilt and shame through temporary palliatives, but these cannot provide lasting relief. The only permanent solution for guilt is to acknowledge that Jesus paid for our sins with His own blood, and to receive God's forgiveness on that basis. At times, like Zacchaeus in Luke 19, we may also have to make restitution.

Shame is more complex than guilt because it attacks our identity, not just our actions. It tells us that *we* are defective. But even with shame, the only real solution is Jesus' work on the cross, which declares how deeply God loves and values us. Romans 5:8 states this in no uncertain terms.

Our Lord's final discourse concludes with these words:

> I have told you these things, so that in me you may have peace. In this world you will have trouble. But take heart! I have overcome the world. (John 16:33 NIV)

Since John is the last Gospel, sequentially and chronologically, these are Jesus' last recorded words to His disciples before His death and resurrection. Given the context, the term "these things" can be taken to refer to His *entire teaching*, not merely what He has just said. And the conjunction "so that" is equally significant. It implies that the purpose of Jesus' teaching was *so that in Him we would have peace.*

READ: Matthew 28
REFLECT: John 16:33
PRAY: Think of an issue for which you need inward peace and receive it from the Lord today.

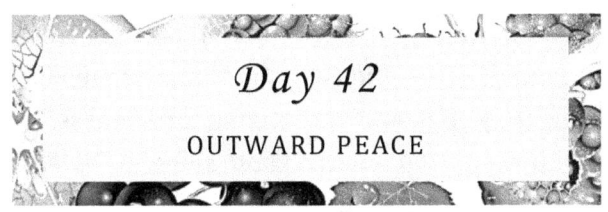

Day 42
OUTWARD PEACE

Peace with others, in its truest sense, can only come from the One who has bridged the ultimate chasm of enmity—the chasm that existed between us and God. As those who are no longer God's enemies, we are to live peaceably with those outside of Christ as well as with our fellow believers.

The epistles abound with exhortations to live in such a manner. For example, when Paul discusses the issue of unbelieving spouses, he sums it up by saying, "God has called us to live in peace" (1 Cor. 7:15 NIV). When he addresses how we are to walk worthy of our calling as members of Christ's body, he implores us to be "eager to maintain the unity of the Spirit in the bond of peace" (Eph. 4:3 ESV). Thus, since peace is God's will for us, and since it preserves the unity of the Spirit, it should characterize all our relationships.

At one point in the Sermon on the Mount Jesus says,

> If you are offering your gift at the altar and there remember that your brother has something against you, leave your gift there before the altar and go. First be reconciled to your brother, and then come and offer your gift. (Matt. 5:23–24 ESV)

This tells us that our gifts are not as important to God as our being in right relationship with our family, biological and spiritual. The word for reconciled in Matthew 5: 24, *diallasso*, means to renew friendship, and that requires more than a perfunctory apology or shrugging off the offense as "nothing." It means admitting that a wrong was done and exchanging forgiveness. Reconciliation also requires a willingness on *both* sides, for *diallasso* carries the sense of mutual concession.

The essence of what Jesus is saying in Matthew 5:23–24 is that we must keep ourselves free of an unforgiving spirit, because the basis of our relationship with God is that He has forgiven us. It is not insignificant that immediately after teaching what we call the Lord's Prayer, Jesus has this to say:

> If you forgive other people when they sin against you, your heavenly Father will also forgive you. But if you do not forgive others their sins, your Father will not forgive your sins. (Matt. 6:14–15 NIV)

The importance of forgiveness is reiterated in Matthew 18, where Peter asks, "Lord, how often shall my brother sin against me, and I forgive him? Up to seven times?" (v. 21). The reply he receives is, "Up to seventy times seven" (v. 22).

By this Jesus does not mean a literal 490 times. He is using a figure of speech to mean *always. Whenever* we need to forgive our brother or sister, we must forgive. And we do this because of how much God has forgiven us. To drive home the point, Jesus follows up His reply with the parable of the unforgiving servant.

READ: Romans 1
REFLECT: Ephesians 4:32
PRAY: Think of someone you need to forgive and ask the Lord to help you forgive them as He has forgiven you.

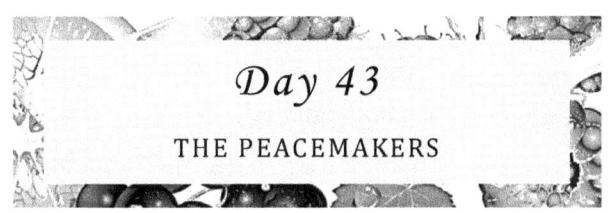

Day 43

THE PEACEMAKERS

The seventh Beatitude is a benediction on those who pursue peace: "Blessed are the peacemakers, for they will be called the children of God" (Matt. 5:9). We noted on Day 24 that seven represents divine perfection; and a few verses later Jesus Himself will say, "You therefore must *be perfect*, as your heavenly Father is perfect" (v. 48 ESV). The word used, *teleois*, does not mean flawless but complete, mature, and *that which reaches its aim*.

Since peacemaking is an attribute of God, peacemakers will be called His *children*. As children resemble their parents, we must resemble our heavenly Father in our desire to make peace. Jesus, the Son of God, is the great Peacemaker, and He is just like His Father.

It must be stressed that Jesus has blessed the peace*makers*, not the peace*keepers*. Peacemakers are needed in times of war and conflict; peacekeepers are needed afterwards. Peacekeepers simply enforce what someone else has initiated, but peacemakers themselves do the initiating. Jesus calls us to be the latter. Paul advises that *as far as it depends on us*, we must live at peace with everyone (Rom. 12:18). And the writer of Hebrews instructs us to *pursue* peace with all (Heb. 12:14). Thus, our part in the peacemaking process is meant to be an active one.

Peacekeeping is indispensable in international affairs, but in the interpersonal realm it is often the fear of man in disguise. Sometimes when we act "for the sake of peace," it may be stemming from the fear of man, for we are afraid of what others will think. But the fear of man is a bondage: it "will prove to be a snare" (Prov. 29:25).

The fear of man keeps us enslaved to the opinion of others, and the opinion of others is anything but constant. The only constant is that it is constantly changing! People are forever adjusting their opinion of us. If we base our peace on what people think of us, we will be sure to lose it before long. A more serious consequence is that the fear of man keeps us from fearing *the Lord*.

The fear of the Lord is to love, trust, honor, and obey Him above all. Solomon describes it as "the beginning of wisdom" (Prov. 9:10), and "a fountain of life, turning a person away from the snares of death" (Prov. 14:27 NIV).

To fear the Lord is to live by what He thinks rather than by what anyone else thinks. No matter how upright and honorable that other person might be, they will not be the final judge of our lives. And no matter how much power they may have, they are not all-powerful: as Solomon has also said, "When a man's ways please the LORD, He makes *even his enemies* to be at peace with him" (Prov. 16:7).

READ: Romans 2
REFLECT: Proverbs 9:10
PRAY: Ask the Lord to free you from the fear of man and to increase in you the fear of the Lord today.

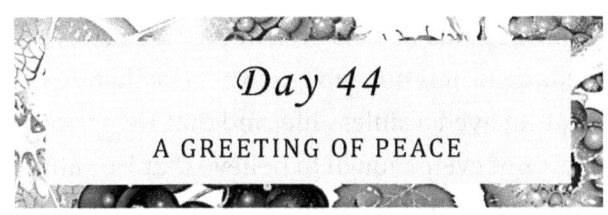

Day 44

A GREETING OF PEACE

On Day 3 we noted that in Jewish culture the word *shalom* is used in greeting and in farewell, and Jesus uses it in both ways. As a greeting, the most famous instance occurs on the evening after He has risen.

Fearing the world's reaction to the empty tomb, the disciples are huddled together in a closed room when Jesus appears in their midst and greets them in these words: "Peace be with you" (John 20:19). He shows them His hands and His side and repeats His greeting: "Peace to you" (v. 21). Jesus reappears eight days later and again greets the disciples in the same manner: "Peace to you" (v. 26).

On this occasion Thomas is also present. Earlier this disciple had declared that unless he saw and touched the imprint of nails in Jesus' hands, he would not believe that He had risen. Now the Lord tells him to see and touch. Satisfied with what his eyes tell him, Thomas no longer needs to touch and instead utters a cry of worship.

Jesus responds with a gentle rebuke. "Because you have seen Me, you have believed," He says. "Blessed are those who have not seen and yet have believed" (John 20:29). Based on the context, our Lord is specifically blessing those who believe *in His resurrection*.

Everything stands or falls on whether we believe that Jesus rose from the dead. It is not enough to believe that He was born of a virgin, that He lived a sinless life, and that He performed many miracles. It is not even enough to believe that He suffered on the cross for our sins. Unless we believe that He died *and vanquished death by rising again*, our faith is not of eternal value. As Paul says, "If only for this life we have hope in Christ, we are of all people most to be pitied" (1 Cor. 15:19 NIV). In fact, he went so far as to say that if Christ has not been raised, we are still in our sins and our faith is "futile" (v. 17).

Our spiritual ancestor Abraham believed in the resurrection, as we know from two passages. The first, Romans 4:17–19, is with reference to the birth of Isaac. Even though Abraham and Sarah's reproductive systems were "already dead" (v. 19), Abraham believed that God "gives life to the dead" (v. 17). He believed this more than he believed the fact of his and Sarah's biological condition, and he eventually became the father of Isaac.

The context of the second passage, Hebrews 11:17–19, is the best-known example of Abraham's faith: the binding of Isaac. Abraham laid his son on the altar believing that "God could raise the dead" (v. 19 NIV), and that's what happened—figuratively to Isaac but literally to Jesus, the greatest Son of Abraham. Since Abraham is the father of all who believe, all who believe must believe in the resurrection.

READ: Romans 3
REFLECT: Romans 10:9
PRAY: Thank the Lord that He rose from the dead and pray for the salvation of someone you know.

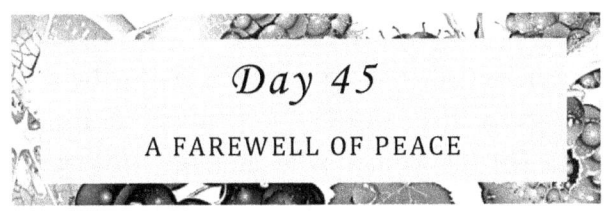

Day 45

A FAREWELL OF PEACE

As a term of farewell, Jesus says shalom to two nameless women. To the one who anointed His feet in the home of Simon the Pharisee, Jesus says, "Your faith has saved you. Go in peace" (Luke 7:50). To the one who touched the hem of His garment He says, "Your faith has made you well. Go in peace" (Luke 8:48).

In both instances, before Jesus confers a benediction of peace, He commends the woman for her faith, for it was her faith that got her what she needed. The sinful woman needed forgiveness, the hemorrhaging woman needed healing, and both miracles were obtained by faith. The actions of anointing Jesus' feet and touching the hem of His garment were prompted by pure, wholehearted faith, and that faith catapults these women into the elite company of the people whose faith Jesus publicly commended.

As we saw on Day 2, the Hebrew verb for bless, *barak*, means to kneel. Kneeling is the posture that most strongly conveys humility, and it is thus an appropriate posture to assume when we are seeking God's blessings. It is primarily an attitude of the heart, but the two women in Luke quite literally knelt before Jesus. To anoint His feet and to touch the hem of His garment, they would have had to get down on their knees. And down on their knees, they got not only a miracle but also a blessing.

When He tells the women "Go in peace," Jesus is not dismissing them from His presence so much as giving them an intimation of their new life—and that new life is radically different from the old. For the woman who anointed His feet, the old life was one of sin; for the woman who touched the hem of His garment, it was one of sickness and poverty. But one encounter with the Prince of Peace, one act of pure, wholehearted faith, and everything changed!

Another similarity between these women is that they were both ritually unclean, one by her lifestyle, the other by her hemorrhage. Neither could go to the synagogue and receive the priestly blessing; but by coming to Jesus they received a blessing infinitely greater than what any Levitical priest could bestow.

As we examine the priesthood of Jesus in the days ahead, it will be helpful to bear in mind that what was true of those two nameless women can be true of us. We can daily come to our great High Priest by faith. He is ever willing to cleanse, forgive, heal, and bless us as He did the women, so that we too can step into the next moment—or *go*—in peace.

> READ: Romans 4
> REFLECT: John 14:27
> PRAY: Ask the Lord to help you do one act of pure, wholehearted faith today.

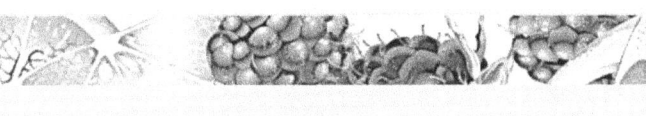

Part Three

THE PRIEST

The LORD said to my Lord,
"Sit at My right hand,
Till I make Your enemies Your footstool."
The LORD shall send the rod of Your strength
    out of Zion.
Rule in the midst of Your enemies!
Your people shall be volunteers
In the day of Your power;
In the beauties of holiness, from the womb
    of the morning
You have the dew of Your youth.
The LORD has sworn
And will not relent,
"You are a priest forever
According to the order of Melchizedek."

—PSALM 110:1–4

But [Jesus], because He continues forever, has an unchangeable priesthood. Therefore He is also able to save to the uttermost those who come to God through Him, since He always lives to make intercession for them.

—HEBREWS 7:24–25

Fruitful Days
46–61

Day 46

PRIEST OF GOD MOST HIGH

The verse in which Melchizedek is introduced, Genesis 14:18, gives us the first mention of the word priest in the Bible. And not only is he the first priest mentioned in Scripture, but Melchizedek is also most closely related to Jesus *as a priest*. The writer of Hebrews devotes a whole chapter to this theme.

To understand how Jesus' priesthood is like that of Melchizedek, we must refer back to the institution of priesthood. The first priests of Israel are mentioned in Exodus 19, just before the Lord gives the Ten Commandments. But before that can happen, He makes what is known as the Mosaic covenant:

> If you will indeed obey My voice and keep My covenant, then you shall be a special treasure to Me above all people; for all the earth is Mine. And you shall be to Me a kingdom of priests and a holy nation. (Ex. 19:5-6)

From the wording of the Mosaic covenant we learn that God's desire for Israel is to make them not simply a kingdom but a kingdom *of priests*. Just as Jesus does not want servants but disciples, God the Father does not want His kingdom filled with subjects but with *priests*. Peter was probably remembering the words of the Mosaic covenant when he told the church:

> You are a chosen generation, a royal priesthood, a holy nation, His own special people, that you may proclaim the

praises of Him who called you out of darkness into His marvelous light. (1 Pet. 2:9)

On the third day after the Mosaic covenant, the Lord descends on Mount Sinai and tells Moses, "Let the priests who come near the LORD consecrate themselves, lest the LORD break out against them" (Ex. 19:22). These priests have never been mentioned before and we are not told when their ministry began; but the first time God mentions them, He refers to the priests as those who *come near the Lord*. This indicates that the priestly functions of worship and intercession cannot be done from afar.

Equally significant is the instruction God has for the priests: *they must consecrate themselves*. In the wilderness, consecration involved physical cleansing—including washing clothes and abstaining from sex. For us in the new covenant, it means approaching God through the blood of Jesus, which cleanses us from all sin (1 John 1:7).

To consecrate something is to set it apart or sanctify it, and we are urged to "sanctify the Lord God in [our] hearts" (1 Pet. 3:15). This means that the Lord must have the most special place in our lives, a place of honor that surpasses all other appetites, affections, and allegiances.

> *READ: Romans 5*
> *REFLECT: 1 Peter 2:9*
> *PRAY: Thank the Lord for calling you out of darkness into His light, and share your testimony with someone today.*

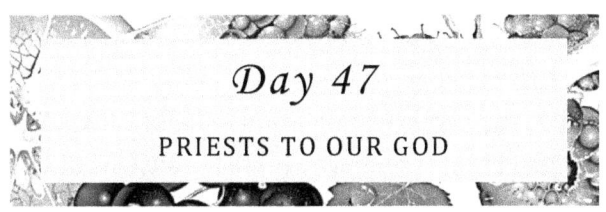

Day 47
PRIESTS TO OUR GOD

According to the command God gave to Moses in Numbers 8, the Israelite priesthood was reserved for the tribe of Levi. The Lord later refers to the priesthood as "My covenant with Levi" (Mal. 2: 4), and Nehemiah will speak of "the covenant of the priesthood and the Levites" (Neh. 13:29).

The name Levi means *attached*. When Jacob's third son was born, his mother hoped that at last her husband would become attached to her (Gen. 29:34). Although Jacob never became attached to any woman except Rachel, Leah had given her third son a prophetic name, for it is the priest who joins a man and woman in matrimony. In spiritual terms, it was the priest who united the people of Israel to their divine Husband. God Himself played on the name Levi when He told Aaron that the Levites would be "joined with" him for the work of the sanctuary (Num. 18:2–3).

Apart from his name, Levi's birth order is also symbolic. He was born between Simeon, meaning *hearing*, and Judah, meaning *praise*. This suggests that the priests must help people to hear God's words as well as to praise Him.

When the Levites revered God and truth was on their lips, they walked "in peace and uprightness, and turned many from sin" (Mal. 2:6 NIV). This is the duty of all priests: "For the lips of a priest ought to preserve knowledge, because he is the messenger of the LORD Almighty and people seek instruction from his mouth" (v. 7 NIV).

Zacharias, the last priest mentioned before the birth of Jesus, the great High Priest, is rendered mute because he did not believe the words of the angel Gabriel. Later, when his lips are opened, he is filled with the Spirit and prophesies about his son John's ministry, and that "the Dayspring from on high" will "give light to those who sit in darkness and the shadow of death" (Luke 1:78-79). The healing of Zacharias's lips is a powerful story of God's "abundant redemption" (Ps. 130:7).

The Levitical priesthood was "a gift, given by the LORD, to do the work of the tabernacle" (Num. 18:6). The priestly duties included offering sacrifices, burning incense, maintaining the sanctuary, and keeping the lamp burning. The priests also blessed the people, purified the unclean, and taught the law.

Like the Levites, we are to offer *the sacrifice of praise* (Col. 3:16; Heb. 13:15) and *prayers*, which are like incense (Matt. 9:38; Eph. 6:18; 1 Thess. 5:17; 1 Tim. 2:1-2; James 5:14-15; Rev. 5:8). We must also *keep our body holy*, for it is the temple of the living God (1 Cor. 6:19-20), and *keep the lamp of witness burning* (Matt. 5:14-16; Luke 12:35). Our other priestly duties include *blessing people*, even those who persecute us (Luke 6:28; Rom. 12:14,17); *cleansing ourselves* from all defilement and from an evil conscience (2 Cor. 7:1; Heb. 10:22); and *teaching others what pleases God* (Matt. 28:20; 2 Tim. 2:2).

> *READ: Romans 6*
> *REFLECT: 1 Thessalonians 5:17*
> *PRAY: Pick one priestly duty listed in the last paragraph and ask the Holy Spirit to help you perform it today.*

Day 48
A KINGDOM OF PRIESTS

When the door of heaven opens in Revelation 4, John sees the Lord God Almighty seated on the throne, holding in His right hand a scroll with seven seals. The Lion of the tribe of Judah takes the scroll from God's hand, at which the living creatures and the elders fall down before Him and sing a new song:

> Worthy are you to take the scroll and to open its seals, for you were slain, and by your blood you ransomed people for God from every tribe and language and people and nation, and you have made them a kingdom and priests to our God, and they shall reign on the earth. (Rev. 5:9–10 ESV)

The song was no doubt echoing in John's thoughts when he wrote the doxology in Revelation 1:

> To him who loves us and has freed us from our sins by his blood and made us a kingdom, priests to his God and Father, to him be glory and dominion forever and ever. Amen. (vv. 5–6 ESV)

According to the song and the doxology, the eternal destiny of the redeemed is for us to be priests to God and to reign on the earth. We will not be floating about aimlessly, wearing haloes and bearing harps. Instead, we will lead busy, purposeful lives as nothing less than priests and rulers! If we will keep this eternal destiny always in view, our brief span on earth will be infused with meaning and purpose. It will also allow us to serve others without complaining or feeling ashamed, for we know that even our Lord "did not come to be served, but to serve, and to give His life a ransom for many" (Mark 10:45).

When God made the Mosaic covenant, promising to make the Israelites a kingdom of priests, they initially accepted its terms: in unison they responded, "We will do everything the LORD has said" (Ex. 19:8). But three days later, after God finishes giving the Ten Commandments, the people renege from fear. "Speak to us yourself and we will listen," they tell Moses. "But do not have God speak to us or we will die" (Ex. 20:19 NIV).

What would have made them a kingdom of priests was hearing the voice of God, but they rejected the offer. Perhaps they were daunted by the effort it would involve, and perhaps they lacked the desire.

Even though we live under the new covenant, the same terms apply to us: to be a kingdom of priests we must hear the voice of God. This requires that we know both the Scriptures and the power of God (Mark 12:24). Additionally, what was said of the early apostles in Acts 4:13 should be true of us: like them, we too must be those who have "been with Jesus."

READ: Romans 7
REFLECT: Mark 10:45
PRAY: Thank the Lord for the ways that He serves you and ask Him to help you selflessly serve someone today.

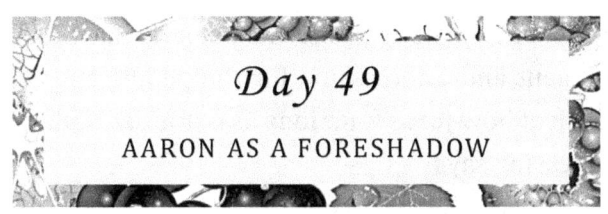

Day 49

AARON AS A FORESHADOW

Israel's first high priest typifies Jesus, our great High Priest, in at least four ways.

First, *Aaron's rod* foreshadows Jesus' election and authority. To confirm Aaron's priestly appointment the Lord tells Moses to get a rod from each tribe and write Aaron's name on the rod of Levi. "The rod of the man I choose will blossom," He says (Num. 17:5). As it turns out, Aaron's rod not only buds and blossoms but also produces ripe almonds!

The word for rod, *mattah*, is the same word David uses in Psalm 110:2, when he prophesies, "The LORD shall send the rod of Your strength out of Zion." *Mattah* is used variously of a branch for chastising, a scepter for ruling, and a staff for walking. It is thus applicable to Jesus, who is the One to whom the Father has committed all judgment (John 5:22), who is the King of kings (Rev. 19:16), and who is the One we lean on throughout our life, even when we walk through the valley of the shadow of death (Ps. 23:4).

Second, *Aaron's priestly garments*, described in detail in Exodus 28, symbolize his role as mediator between God and Israel. As such, they point to Jesus' intermediary role: "For there is one God, and one mediator also between God and men, the man Christ Jesus" (1 Tim. 2:5 NASB).

Third, *Aaron's priestly duties*, particularly his duties of making atonement and intercession for the people and of blessing them, speak of how Jesus functions as our great High Priest. The Aaronic blessing says:

> The LORD bless you and keep you;
> The LORD make His face to shine upon you.
> And be gracious to you;
> The LORD lift up His countenance to you,
> And give you peace. (Num. 6:24–26)

In Christ, these blessings are ours. He blesses us by helping us turn from sin (Acts 3:26), and He is able to keep us from falling (Jude 1:24). In Him we have seen the light of God's face (2 Cor. 4:6), we have received grace (John 1:17), and we have peace with God (Rom. 5:1).

Fourth, *Aaron's death* poignantly prefigures Jesus'. He is taken up to Mount Hor and divested of his priestly garments before dying (Num. 20:25–28). Similarly, Jesus was lifted up on the cross on the hill of Golgotha, and stripped of His robe before being crucified (Mark 15:22,24). And just as Aaron's garments were passed on to his heir Eleazar, who became the next high priest, Jesus before ascending into heaven gave His disciples, the heirs of His message, the authority to function as priests. The tasks He has laid out for us in the Great Commission—making disciples by baptizing and teaching—are all *priestly* duties.

READ: Romans 8
REFLECT: Numbers 6:24–26
PRAY: Ask the Lord to give you deeper revelation into one of the Aaronic blessings that is yours in Christ.

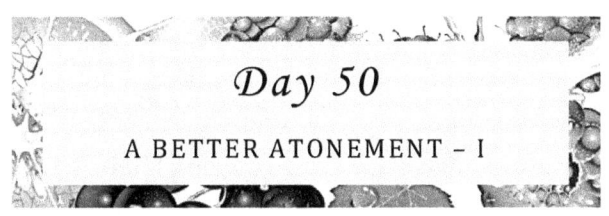

Day 50
A BETTER ATONEMENT – I

The supremacy of Jesus over the Judaic system is the primary theme of Hebrews. His superiority as a priest (Heb. 4:14–7:28) means that the atonement He made is better than Aaron's.

On the Day of Atonement or Yom Kippur, the most sacred day of the Jewish calendar, the high priest would offer the annual sin offering, as commanded in Leviticus 16. He would then enter the Most Holy Place behind the veil, to sprinkle the sacrificial blood on the golden covering of the ark of the covenant, known as the *kapporeth* in Hebrew.

The word *kapporeth* in the Old Testament is traditionally rendered "mercy seat," but it literally means *covering*. It is related to the verb *kaphar*, meaning to cover or wipe out, which is what the sacrificial blood does to sins. "Mercy seat" is an evocative metaphor, and it adequately depicts God's willingness to forgive sin out of His great mercy, but *kapporeth* is actually the place of covering or atonement.

The people were commanded to observe Yom Kippur as "a sabbath of solemn rest" (Lev. 16:31); and when the writer of Hebrews urges his readers to "be diligent to enter that rest" (Heb. 4:11), he is referring to the rest provided by the atonement Jesus has made on our behalf. We don't have to work to earn our forgiveness, but we must be diligent to receive it.

The atonement Jesus made is superior to Aaron's in at least four ways, the first of which we will consider today.

Whereas Aaron could only offer the sacrifices of animals, Jesus made atonement *with His own blood* (Heb. 9:12). Blood is required for making atonement because "without the shedding of blood there is no remission" (v. 22). The penalty of sin is death (Rom. 6:23), and blood represents life. That is why blood alone can atone for sin.

While making His covenant with Noah God had said, "You shall not eat flesh with its life, *that is, its blood*" (Gen. 9:4). Centuries later, after instituting the Day of Atonement in the wilderness, God tells Moses: "The life of a creature is in the blood, and I have given it to you to make atonement for yourselves on the altar; *it is the blood that makes atonement for one's life*" (Lev. 17:11).

The sacrifices of the old covenant merely *foreshadowed* the atonement Jesus would make with His own blood. Had they been able to permanently deal with the problem of sin, our Lord would not have needed to suffer as He did; but the blood of animals can never take away sin (Heb. 10:4,11). The very fact that the sacrifices had to be repeated annually indicates their inability to "put away sin" (Heb. 9:26). That is why in his great repentance psalm David, who lived under the old covenant, says that the sacrifices of God are not burnt offerings but "a broken spirit and a contrite heart" (Ps. 51:17).

READ: Romans 12

REFLECT: Psalm 51:10

PRAY: *Ask the Lord to cleanse you of any sin you may be harboring in your heart, including the sin of unbelief.*

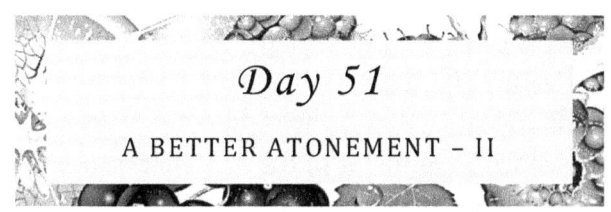

Day 51

A BETTER ATONEMENT - II

Jesus' atonement is also superior to Aaron's because *He Himself was without sin*. Aaron had to make atonement for his own sins as well as those of others (Heb. 9:7), but Jesus did not have any of His own sins to atone for, being "holy, innocent, unstained, [and] separated from sinners" (Heb. 7:26 ESV).

Jesus also made atonement *once for all* (Heb. 7:27; 10:10). Whereas the Aaronic high priest had to make atonement once a year, Yom Kippur after Yom Kippur, Jesus, with one sacrifice of Himself, "obtained eternal redemption" (Heb. 9:12). Moreover, His sacrifice was for all humanity. The Jewish high priest could only make atonement for those in the land of Israel, but Jesus "taste[d] death for everyone" (Heb. 2:9). As He Himself said, "I, when I am lifted up from the earth, will draw *all people* to myself" (John 12:32 NIV).

The universality of Jesus' atonement is reiterated throughout the New Testament. For instance, Paul says that He "gave Himself as a ransom for all" (1 Tim. 2:6). Peter affirms that He "died for sins once for all" (1 Pet. 3:18 NASB). And John says that Jesus is "the atoning sacrifice for our sins, *and not only for ours but also for the sins of the whole world*" (1 John 2:2 NIV). That's how truly inclusive Jesus' atonement is, though each of us must still receive it for ourselves by faith.

Finally, Jesus' atonement is superior to Aaron's because *He does not minister in an earthly temple but in the heavenly one.* Our great High Priest is "seated at the right hand of the throne of the Majesty in heaven, a minister in the holy places, in the true tent that the Lord set up" (Heb. 8:1–2 ESV).

Since the tabernacle erected by Moses was a copy of the heavenly tabernacle, the Most Holy Place in that tabernacle—and later in the Temple—was also only a copy. The true Holiest Place is "the throne of the Majesty in heaven." Whereas the Aaronic high priest could only enter the Holy Place in the earthly tabernacle once a year, Jesus entered the one in heaven for all time (Heb. 9:24–25).

Our great High Priest "has passed through the heavens" and He can "sympathize with our weaknesses" since He "was in all points tempted as we are, yet without sin" (Heb. 4:14–15). This is why we can "come boldly to the throne of grace, that we may obtain mercy and find grace to help in time of need" (v. 16).

According to a popular definition, God's grace is His giving us what we don't deserve, and His mercy is His *not* giving us what we *do* deserve. Thus these two terms run the gamut of God's blessings: as David writes in Psalm 103, He both "satisfies [our] desires with good things" and He "does not treat us as our sins deserve" (vv. 5,10 NIV). To obtain the fruitfulness that God has for us, we must continually approach God to receive the twin blessings of mercy and grace.

READ: Romans 13
REFLECT: Hebrews 4:16
PRAY: Think of something for which you need either mercy or grace today, and ask God for it.

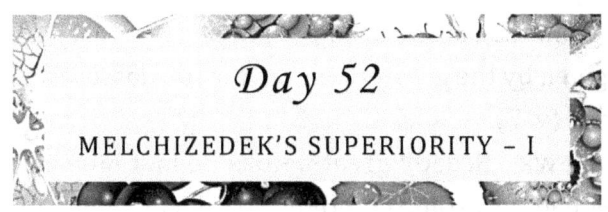

Day 52

MELCHIZEDEK'S SUPERIORITY - I

Melchizedek's name appears for the first time in the New Testament in Hebrews 5:6, where the writer quotes Psalm 110:4. He repeats that verse when he says that Jesus was "called by God as High Priest 'according to the order of Melchizedek'" (Heb. 5:10). But here the writer seems to remember that his readers lack the maturity to understand the typology because they have become "dull of hearing" (v. 11). A homily on spiritual maturity follows, and the priesthood subject is resumed at the end of chapter 6.

Jesus' priesthood is likened to that of Melchizedek in seven ways in Hebrews 7. In the interest of clarity, I will begin with the most obvious point. The rest of the list is ordered by how one point leads to the next rather than by the sequence in Hebrews 7. We must bear in mind that Melchizedek is being used *typologically*, and the discussion is not about him so much as it is about *Jesus*. The writer's purpose is not to explore the identity of Melchizedek but to establish how Jesus, as a priest in the order of Melchizedek and not of Aaron, is superior to the Levitical priesthood. This is one aspect of Jesus' supremacy over the Judaic system, which is the primary theme of Hebrews, as we noted on Day 50.

The first and most obvious way in which Melchizedek establishes his superiority is by blessing Abram when he was "returning from the slaughter of the kings" (Heb. 7:1). Blessing is always given by the greater person, for "the lesser is blessed by the better" (v. 7).

Abram was already great before he met Melchizedek because he "had the promises" (Heb. 7:6); but as king of Salem, Melchizedek was superior to Abram, who was merely an immigrant in the land of Canaan. And since Abram was greater than Levi and Aaron, being their forefather, it follows that *Melchizedek* was also greater than Levi and Aaron.

Next, Melchizedek's greatness is established by the fact that he received Abram's tithes, which the writer of Hebrews specifies was "a tenth of the spoils" (Heb. 7:4). Aaron's ancestor Levi was not yet born when this happened. Thus, although the Levites receive tithes, Levi figuratively *paid* tithes to Melchizedek, through his forefather Abraham (vv. 9–10).

Since tithes are always given *to* the superior person, Abram's tithe proves that Melchizedek was greater than Abram and therefore also than his descendants Levi and Aaron. Furthermore, whereas the Levites receive tithes from their fellow Israelites, who are their brethren, Melchizedek received tithes from the Levites' *patriarch*. This further emphasizes the superiority of Melchizedek's—and therefore *Jesus's*—priesthood over that of Aaron.

READ: Romans 14
REFLECT: Colossians 2:9–10
PRAY: Ask the Holy Spirit to deepen your understanding of Jesus' priesthood and how it applies to you today.

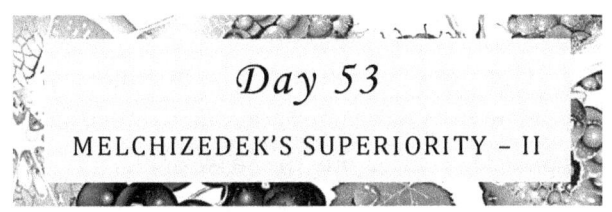

Day 53
MELCHIZEDEK'S SUPERIORITY - II

When the writer says that Melchizedek was "without father, without mother, without genealogy, having neither beginning of days nor end of life" (Heb. 7:3), he means that we have no record of Melchizedek's lifespan or genealogy. By contrast, we know that Aaron's parents were Levites named Amram and Jochebed, and his siblings were Miriam and Moses (Num. 26:59). Scripture also mentions the names of Aaron's wife and sons (Ex. 6:23). Furthermore, we are told that he was born three years before Moses (Ex. 7:7), and he died at 123, on the first day of the fifth month of the fortieth year after the exodus (Num. 33:38–39). These details, and the corresponding lack of material on Melchizedek, point to Jesus' eternal existence.

Like Melchizedek, our Lord also has no beginning of days or end of life. His earthly life began six months after John the Baptist was born, yet John himself testifies to Jesus' preexistence: "This is He of whom I said, 'He who comes after me has a higher rank than I, *for He existed before me*'" (John 1:15 NASB). Aaron's life began at conception, as ordinary human lives do, but Jesus has always existed: as John 1:2 says, "He was with God in the beginning." And whereas Aaron died and stayed dead, Jesus rose from the dead. He "will never die again [for] death no longer has dominion over him" (Rom. 6:9 ESV).

Hebrews 7:3 also says that Melchizedek "remains a priest continually." This does not mean that he operates as a priest today (unless of course he was a preincarnate appearance of Jesus). Rather, the phrase is conveying the *sense of eternity* that characterizes Melchizedek and his priesthood, mostly to contrast it to the temporality of Aaron and his priesthood.

Melchizedek is frozen in time as a priest because we only saw him function as a priest. We have not seen him judging a case or going to war or building an ark. We only have that one priestly act to remember him by. And while he may have died and stayed dead (unless he was Jesus), there is no record of his death. This further emphasizes the sense of eternity.

By contrast, we saw Aaron before he became a priest—the first time as a slave in Egypt, in fact—and his death is recorded in Numbers 20. His priesthood was passed to his son Eleazar, and then to *his* son, Phinehas. Death prevented Aaron and every subsequent Levitical priest from continuing in office (Heb. 7:23), but Jesus defeated death by rising again. He has "an unchangeable priesthood" and He "continues forever" (v. 24).

Because Jesus has an unchangeable priesthood, He "always lives to make intercession" for those who come to God through Him and He can save them "to the uttermost" (v. 25). The Greek word for uttermost, *panteles*, means complete, forever, and entirely. This tells us that Jesus' priesthood is always in effect, it covers everything for which atonement is required, and it covers to the full extent.

> READ: *John 1*
> REFLECT: *Hebrews 7:25*
> PRAY: *Think of a difficult situation—in your life or in the world at large—and pray Hebrews 7:25 over it.*

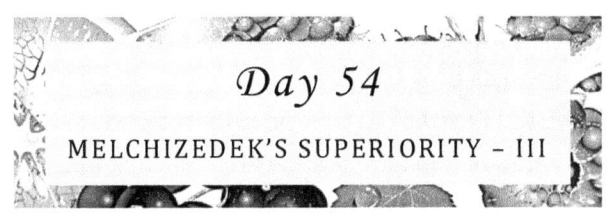

Day 54
MELCHIZEDEK'S SUPERIORITY – III

Aaron derived his priesthood by his descent from Levi, but human descent has nothing to do with Jesus' priesthood. Instead, like Melchizedek, whose priesthood was "without genealogy" (Heb. 7:3), our Lord's priesthood is independent of genealogy, for He descended from the tribe of Judah, "from which no man has officiated at the altar" (v. 13). Genealogy would have disqualified Jesus from priesthood—*unless His priesthood was of a different order than Aaron's*.

The law was given under the Levitical priesthood, and the priesthood itself was the outcome of a commandment God gave Moses in Numbers 8. Melchizedek's priesthood, by contrast, was not given by any known law, which is implicit in the fact that we are not told when it began. We simply see him as a priest. More significantly, *Jesus'* priesthood was "not according to the law of a fleshly commandment, but according to the power of an endless life" (Heb. 7:16).

A commandment is always given by a higher authority to a subordinate, as was the command God gave Moses for the institution of the Levitical priesthood. Power, on the other hand, comes from within. The Greek word *dunamis* speaks of *inherent power*, the power that resides within a person or thing. That is what Jesus' priesthood is founded upon.

The final aspect of Melchizedek's *and especially of Jesus'* superiority concerns how the Aaronic priesthood was initiated. As noted above, the Levites became priests by a command God gave Moses, whereas we don't know how Melchizedek became a priest. More importantly, we know that *Jesus* became a priest by an oath God made directly to Him. To support the point that "He was not made priest without an oath" (Heb. 7:20), the writer quotes Psalm 110:4.

Hebrews 7 concludes with this verse: "The law appoints as high priests men who have weakness, but the word of oath, which came after the law, appoints the Son" (v. 28). We know that Jesus is the Son of God, and thus the discussion comes full circle, for at the outset of the chapter the writer had said Melchizedek was "made like the Son of God" (v. 3). Hebrews 7:28 also harks back to the start of the epistle, where we are told that "in these last days [God has] spoken to us by His Son, whom He has appointed heir of all things" (Heb. 1:2).

In the homily sandwiched between Hebrews 7 and the invocation of Melchizedek's name in Hebrews 5, the writer had said, "When God made the promise to Abraham, *since He could swear by no one greater, He swore by Himself*" (Heb. 6:13 NASB). God is the supreme authority in the universe, and His word is His bond. What He has promised to do, He *will* do, for "it is impossible for God to lie" (v. 18). That is why, when the Father promised His Son an eternal priesthood according to the order of Melchizedek, *His Son got it.*

> READ: *John 2*
> REFLECT: *Numbers 23:19–20*
> PRAY: *Thank the Lord that He keeps His promises and ask Him to forgive you for the times you have doubted Him.*

Day 55
THE IDENTITY OF MELCHIZEDEK

According to some rabbinical traditions, Melchizedek is Noah's son Shem, but this theory does not hold water when examined against the biblical book with the most references to Melchizedek. The writer of Hebrews, who was well-versed in Jewish history and also writing under divine inspiration, tells us that Melchizedek was "without father, without mother, without genealogy, having neither beginning nor end of life" (Heb. 7:3).

The Greek words *apator*, *ametor*, and *agenealogetos* in this verse refer to one whose parents are not listed in the genealogies, and whose descent cannot be traced because of the lack of record, not lack of parents. This is Melchizedek's case. By contrast, we know that Shem's parents were Noah and his wife, and his genealogy is listed in Genesis 5, 1 Chronicles 1, and Luke 3.

Nor does identifying Melchizedek as Shem explain his having "neither beginning nor end of life." He was born when Noah was at least 500 (Gen. 5:32), and himself lived 500 years after begetting Arphaxad two years after the Flood (Gen. 11:10–11). Thus, Shem had a beginning and an end of life.

Hebrews 7:3 also tells us that Melchizedek was "made like the Son of God." Nowhere does the Bible say this of Shem. If it had been true, it would have been mentioned in the New Testament, where the Son of God is revealed in His fullness.

There are two possible reasons why Melchizedek was "made like the Son of God." Either he *was* the Son of God, or God wanted someone typological of His Son to bless Abraham before he had even one of the descendants through whom the Messiah would come. The first reason may or may not be true, but the second certainly is.

The Messiah would be a king-priest, and He would be greater than Abraham, and the type had to be the same. Melchizedek is the only one who fits the bill. He is both a king and a priest, and he proves his superiority by blessing Abraham and receiving his tithes. Thus, in making Melchizedek "like the Son of God," God had put in place a shadow or type that would someday prove the supremacy of His Son over the entire Judaic system, *including its patriarch*.

Even so, not all Jews are convinced about Jesus' superiority. "Are you greater than our father Abraham?" they ask on one occasion. When Jesus replies "Before Abraham was, I AM" (John 8:58), He is not only declaring Himself to be greater than Abraham but also making Himself equal to God. For this the Jews are ready to stone Him.

We can learn much about the Hebrew roots of our faith from rabbinical literature, and it can shed light on various messianic prophecies, but it cannot teach us about Jesus as the Messiah. For that we must read the Bible in its entirety, especially the New Testament, where Christ is revealed in His fullness, not merely in shadows and types.

> *READ: John 3*
> *REFLECT: John 20:31*
> *PRAY: Ask the Holy Spirit to deepen your understanding of Jesus' greatness, and worship Jesus for it.*

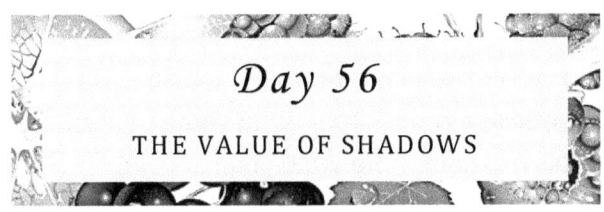

Day 56

THE VALUE OF SHADOWS

The epistles tell us that the former things are shadows and types. For instance, Paul says the festivals and Sabbaths are "a shadow of things to come, but the substance is of Christ" (Col. 2:17). The writer of Hebrews similarly says that the law has "a shadow of the good things to come, and not the very image of the things" (Heb. 10:1). Since we live in the "now" and the "not yet" of the kingdom of God, the "good things" foreshadowed in the Torah include everything Jesus has already brought and all that He will bring when He returns.

Knowing that "the substance is of Christ" does not minimize the value of the shadows. On the contrary, it gives the shadows *an even greater value*. An analogy from literature may help illustrate this point.

A good novelist drops hints about their plot and characters from the very beginning. These hints often elude us when we read the novel for the first time, but they don't cease to matter once we finish the novel. If anything, the hints acquire a new significance, for it's only after we have read the novel that we realize they were hints at all.

It's the same with the Old Testament. After we receive Jesus as our personal Savior, the shadows and types are illuminated and rendered even more meaningful.

In John 5:46 Jesus tells the Jews, "If you believed Moses, you would believe Me, for he wrote about Me." Later, in Acts 3:22 and Acts 7:37, both Peter and Stephen will quote Deuteronomy 18:15, where Moses had said: "The LORD your God will raise up for you a Prophet like me from among your brethren. Him shall you hear in all things." Jesus is the One Moses wrote about, and He is the Prophet like Moses. We have but to compare key aspects of their lives to understand that this is so.

When Jesus appeared to the disciples on the evening after His resurrection, He said, "All things must be fulfilled which were written in the Law of Moses and the Prophets and the Psalms concerning Me" (Luke 24:44). He had been written about not only in the Torah but elsewhere in the Old Testament as well: as David had declared in Psalm 40:7, "In the scroll of the book it is written of me." The writer of Hebrews quotes this verse when discussing Christ's sacrifice in Hebrews 10. Those who trust in that sacrifice will read "the scroll of the book" prophetically and bless God for its many messianic shadows, one of whom is Melchizedek.

In the final analysis, the question is not who Melchizedek was but who *Jesus* is. And God's Word reveals that our Lord is the King of Righteousness, the great High Priest who blesses us as Salem's king-priest had blessed Abram. Scripture may be silent on whether the historical Melchizedek was in fact Jesus, but based on everything Scripture does say, we know that Jesus is the real Melchizedek.

> *READ: John 4*
> *REFLECT: Matthew 16:15–17*
> *PRAY: Pray that everyone will have the chance to hear about Jesus and read the Bible in their own language.*

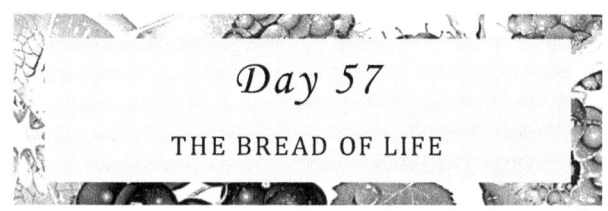

Day 57

THE BREAD OF LIFE

The first thing that Melchizedek does when he meets Abram, even before pronouncing his blessing, is to serve him bread and wine. In Genesis 14:18 we have the first mention of bread and wine together, making Melchizedek's table one of the Torah's many messianic shadows. It points forward to the Lord's Supper, which will memorialize Jesus' atoning work in bread and wine.

Bread and wine are apt symbols of our Lord's suffering, and they also accurately depict the gift of salvation. Like bread that sustains us and wine that gladdens the heart, as Psalm 104:15 says, we *need* salvation and being saved gives us *joy*.

Bread is first mentioned in Scripture right after the Fall, when God tells Adam, "In the sweat of your face you shall eat bread" (Gen. 3:19). Some versions have *food* instead of *bread*, but bread is the original term. The Hebrew word for bread, *lechem*, is part of the name Bethlehem, which means *house of bread*; and Bethlehem, as we know, is the birthplace of the Bread of Life.

In the only miracle recorded in all four Gospels, the feeding of the five thousand, we are told that Jesus blessed the five loaves. Each of the Synoptics uses the word blessed, and although John has "gave thanks," that is a blessing where food is concerned. All four evangelists record the same sequence: our Lord blessed the bread before He broke it. This is significant, for it was only after the bread had been blessed that its breaking would translate into a miracle.

When the people come thronging to Jesus the day after this miracle, He says, "Do not labor for the food which perishes, but for the food which endures to everlasting life" (John 6:27). He adds,

> I am the bread of life. Your fathers ate manna in the wilderness, and are dead.... I am the living bread which came down from heaven. If anyone eats of this bread, he will live forever; and the bread that I shall give is My flesh, which I shall give for the life of the world. (vv. 48–52)

Jesus' audience would have recalled Moses' words about manna. On the threshold of the Promised Land, Moses reminds the Israelites of how God has led them through the wilderness these forty years, giving them manna to eat, to teach them that "man does not live by bread alone but by every word that proceeds from the mouth of the LORD" (Deut. 8:3).

Like the manna that fell from the sky, Jesus came to earth from heaven; but as the living bread, He satisfies our *spiritual* hunger —the hunger that resides in the part of us that will live forever, unlike our mortal bodies. And He satisfies it *always*: as He said, "I am the bread of life. Whoever comes to me will *never* go hungry, and whoever believes in me will *never* be thirsty" (John 6:35 NIV).

READ: John 5
REFLECT: Deuteronomy 8:3
PRAY: Ask God to increase your hunger for Him and His Word and to decrease it for one unwholesome thing.

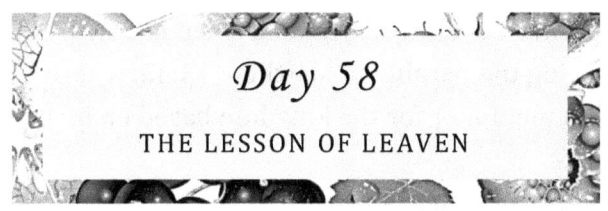

Day 58

THE LESSON OF LEAVEN

After another miracle associated with bread, the feeding of the four thousand, Jesus warns the disciples to guard against "the leaven of the Pharisees and Sadducees" (Matt. 16:6 ESV). The disciples initially think Jesus has alluded to leaven because they don't have bread, so He reminds them of the miracle He has just performed. That is when the disciples understand that Jesus is referring to the *teaching* of the Pharisees and Sadducees.

Both sects held certain incorrect doctrines. For instance, the Sadducees did not believe in the resurrection of the dead, and the Pharisees placed undue emphasis on the oral Torah, which comprised the traditions of the elders or rabbis. But based on the immediate context, what Jesus is warning against is *the teaching that demands signs to test God*, as the Pharisees and Sadducees had just done. This teaching may not be written down, but it's what they teach *by example*—and it has the same corrupting influence on others that leaven has on dough. Later Paul, while cautioning the Galatian church against false doctrines, will say, "A little leaven leavens the whole lump" (Gal. 5:9 ESV).

Leaven is a lump of stale, fermenting dough which, when kneaded into a new batch, causes it to ferment so that the bread will rise. Sin does much the same to a person: it corrupts their life and causes them to puff up with pride and self-importance. In the Bible leaven is always symbolic of sin and evil, the only exception being the parable in Matthew 13:33, where Jesus uses leaven as a metaphor for the kingdom based on its permeating properties.

The Feast of Unleavened Bread, which God had instituted simultaneously with the Passover (Ex. 12:17), contained another messianic shadow: like the unleavened bread or *matzah*, Jesus was without sin and not puffed up with pride. On the contrary, He had humbled Himself by taking on human form and being obedient to death (Phil. 2:7–8), and He was "humble in heart" (Matt. 11:29 NIV).

When Paul had to rebuke the Corinthian church for tolerating sexual immorality, he again quoted the proverb about leaven. Then he added,

> Cleanse out the old leaven that you may be a new lump, as you really are unleavened. For Christ, our Passover Lamb, has been sacrificed. Let us therefore celebrate . . . with the unleavened bread of sincerity and truth. (1 Cor. 5:7–8 ESV)

Paul's word to the Corinthians applies to us all. We have already been cleansed of sin or made "unleavened" by the atoning work of Christ; now we must live in a manner worthy of that sacrifice.

READ: John 6
REFLECT: John 6:63
PRAY: Ask the Lord to show you what He considers "leaven" in your life and to give you the grace to get rid of it.

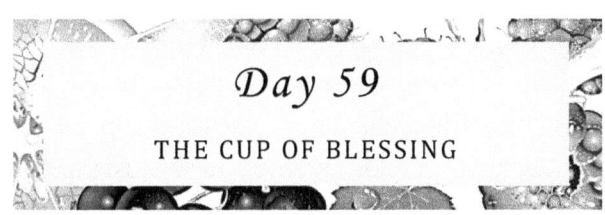

Day 59

THE CUP OF BLESSING

Wine is first mentioned shortly after the Flood, when Noah plants a vineyard (Gen. 9:20–21). This passage contains the first mention of *vineyard*, which Jesus uses in four parables; and in the discourse shortly before His arrest He says, "I am the true vine and My Father is the vinedresser" (John 15:1).

Wine is an apt element in the Lord's Supper because in color it resembles blood. Moreover, just as the grapes are crushed to produce wine, our Lord endured the abject horror of crucifixion to give us eternal life. As the prophet Isaiah had foretold, "He was pierced for our transgressions, he was crushed for our iniquities; the punishment that brought us peace was on him, and by his wounds we are healed" (Is. 53:5 NIV).

The crucifixion took place in the context of Passover, which commemorates the deliverance of the Israelites from Egypt. This event is typological of the deliverance Jesus accomplished for us on the cross. On the evening of the exodus the people killed a lamb without defect and sprinkled its blood on their doorposts. This lamb foreshadows the sinless Lamb of God, whose blood saves us from the fate that befell Egypt's firstborn that night. Thus when John the Baptist sees Jesus approaching him, he declares, "Behold! The Lamb of God who takes away the sin of the world!" (John 1:29).

In 1 Corinthians 10:16, when Paul refers to the communion cup as "the cup of blessing," he is alluding to the Passover seder, at which the cup is filled four times. The third cup, taken after the meal, is known as the cup of redemption or blessing. When Jesus was instituting the Lord's Supper, He took the cup *after* supper (Luke 22:20), which made it the third cup and thus a reference to redemption.

Until the Last Supper, the third cup only recalled the redemption from slavery to Egypt, but on that night it pointed forward to the redemption from human bondage to sin and death, which Jesus was about to provide through His own blood. Today when we take the cup, we are looking *back* to that pivotal event in the story of redemption, the story that both Testaments tell.

In Revelation 12:11, the blood of the Lamb is named as the first of the three means by which we overcome the accuser. Our archenemy is continually levelling charges against us before God on the basis of our sins. God is the righteous judge who will not alter His standard of holiness, and we would be justly incriminated had Jesus not paid for our sins.

The pure and undefiled blood of our great High Priest is the basis by which we approach God—and it is the *only* basis. Everything else is neither legal nor effective. And along with the name of Jesus, His blood is also our most powerful weapon against all the hordes of hell.

READ: John 7
REFLECT: Isaiah 53:5
PRAY: Thank Jesus for the ways in which His stripes have healed you.

Day 60
THE NEW COVENANT

When Jesus served the cup at the Last Supper, He said, "This cup is the new covenant in my blood, which is poured out for you" (Luke 22:20 NIV). This alluded to the prophecy in Jeremiah 31, where God spoke of making a new covenant, one that would be unlike the covenant He had made after delivering the Israelites from Egypt. On that occasion, the people had initially agreed to obey the Lord, but within forty days they were worshiping a golden calf.

The old covenant was faulty because it lacked intimacy. Apart from the fact that the people could not handle hearing God's voice, the terms of the covenant were written on tablets of stone, whereas God wanted them written on His people's *hearts*. This is why He declared of the new covenant,

> I will put my law within them, and I will write it on their hearts. . . . And no longer shall each one teach his neighbor and each his brother, saying, "Know the LORD," for they shall all know me, from the least of them to the greatest, declares the LORD. (Jer. 31:33–34 ESV)

The writer of Hebrews quotes this very passage when speaking about Jesus' superiority over Moses in Hebrews 8.

The new covenant inaugurated by Jesus differs from the old not because we don't need to obey the Lord anymore but because of *how we hear Him*. The law is now written on our hearts. It is internal and intimate. We no longer need a human intermediary to bring God's word to us or to take our response back to Him, as we see Moses doing so often. We have the indwelling Spirit to teach us the written Word and to give us the *rhema* word. As mentioned on Day 1, this is the specific word God speaks to us in specific situations.

At times we all need to receive biblical counsel from our spiritual leaders, but knowing God's will on a day-to-day basis is the responsibility of everyone in the new covenant. Otherwise we are no different from those under the old covenant, who needed Moses, and later the elders and prophets, to continually tell them God's will.

Jesus is superior to Moses because a person is always greater than their shadow, and the covenant He mediates is better. This is why the writer of Hebrews, while contrasting the two covenants, says Jesus has "a more excellent ministry" than Moses, being "the Mediator of a better covenant, which was established on better promises" (Heb. 8:6 NASB). In Jesus we have a "new and living way" to draw near to God:

> Since we have confidence to enter the Most Holy Place by the blood of Jesus, by a new and living way opened for us through the curtain, that is, his body, and since we have a great priest over the house of God, let us draw near to God with a sincere heart and with the full assurance that faith brings. (Heb. 10:19–22 NIV)

READ: John 8
REFLECT: Romans 8:1
PRAY: Think of someone who needs to hear John 8:11 and Romans 8:1 and pray that they will believe it.

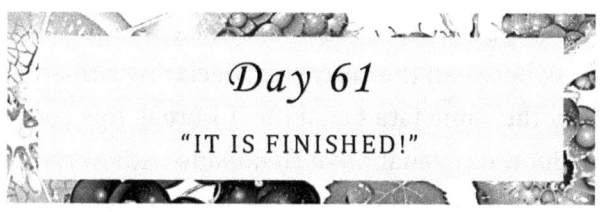

Day 61

"IT IS FINISHED!"

Four hundred years before the Mosaic covenant, God made a covenant with Abram that prefigures the one Jesus would inaugurate at the Last Supper. It takes place shortly after the blessing of Melchizedek and constitutes one of Scripture's most memorable encounters.

In Genesis 15, the Lord appears to Abram in a vision and promises him two things: that he will have a son from his own body, and that his descendants will inherit the land of Canaan. Abram believes the first promise, and his faith is credited to him as righteousness (v. 6). Then God makes the promise about the land. In response Abram asks, "LORD God, how shall I know that I will inherit it?" (v. 8). His faith has not suddenly turned to unbelief; he is simply asking for a land deed or contract. And God is not displeased. In fact, Abram's question is the very cue needed for what will happen next!

The Lord directs Abram to bring five creatures—a heifer, a goat, a ram, a turtledove, and a pigeon—and Abram knows what he must do. Following the ancient Near Eastern practice of covenant-making, he kills the animals and arranges the halves opposite each other. He drives away the raptors that come swooping down and then falls into a deep sleep. That's the extent of his role in the covenant.

A covenant between equals would have required that both parties walk between the carcasses, declaring something to this effect: "May the same fate befall me if I break this covenant between us." But the covenant that God made with Abram had nothing to do with Abram's ability to keep it. That is why Abram slept through the process and God passed between the carcasses alone, in the symbolic form of the smoking oven and the burning torch.

Not only was God's covenant with Abram not made between equals, but it was also not a *contract*. Contracts have expiration dates, they can be broken or revoked, and keeping them depends on the worthiness of both parties. By contrast, God's covenant with Abram depended solely on His own worthiness—and the same is true of the covenant He has made with us. Our part is to trust Him, as Abram did.

God's covenant with Abram is among the earliest foreshadows of the new covenant. Just as Abram could do nothing to make the covenant, we too can do nothing to earn our salvation. Jesus has done it all for us. His one perfect sacrifice of Himself is redemption and atonement enough—forever and for all. This is why in His final moments on the cross, as the breath ebbs from His battered, bleeding body, Jesus lifts His voice in a cry of triumph that will ring throughout time and eternity:

"*It is finished!*"

READ: John 9
REFLECT: Philippians 2:9–11
PRAY: Thank the Lord for the ways that His covenant with Abram foreshadows the one He has made with you.

Part Four

THE BLESSED

And [Melchizedek] blessed [Abram] and said:
"Blessed be Abram of God Most High,
Possessor of heaven and earth.
And blessed be God Most High,
Who has delivered your enemies into your hand."

—GENESIS 14:19–20

Christ has redeemed us from the curse of the law, having become a curse for us (for it is written, "*Cursed is everyone who hangs on a tree*"), that the blessing of Abraham might come upon the Gentiles in Christ Jesus, that we might receive the promise of the Spirit through faith.

—GALATIANS 3:13–14

I heard the voice of many angels around the throne, the living creatures, and the elders; and the number of them was ten thousand times ten thousand, and thousands of thousands, saying with a loud voice:
"Worthy is the Lamb who was slain
To receive power and riches and wisdom,
And strength and honor and glory and blessing!"

—REVELATION 5:11–12

Fruitful Days
62–86

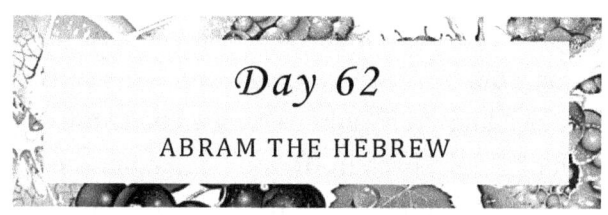

Day 62

ABRAM THE HEBREW

Melchizedek opens by addressing the recipient of his blessing as "Abram of God Most High." The two persons mentioned in this clause—Abram and God—are linked with the preposition "of," which indicates that a person or thing belongs to or is related to another. To appreciate its significance in Genesis 14:19, we must go back a few verses, to what happened after the war of the kings.

When Chedorlaomer king of Elam defeated the kings of Sodom and Gomorrah in the Vale of Siddim, he captured their goods and people, including Lot. One person managed to escape and make it to the oaks of Mamre, to inform "Abram the Hebrew" of Lot's abduction (Gen. 14:13). This is the Bible's first mention of the word Hebrew, and it has something critical to teach us about Abram and the life of faith.

The word Hebrew is derived from the root *eber*, meaning *regions beyond*, and thus refers to *one from the other side*. In the land of Canaan "the other side" typically meant the other side of the Jordan, which is where Abram was from, and it carried the sense of otherness. To be a Hebrew was to be an alien, a stranger, a foreigner.

As we noted on Day 19, in the Bible a person's name usually represented their destiny—specifically, what kind of person they would turn out to be and what they would end up doing with their lives. But while a person's name represented their destiny, their *identity* came from whose child they were. If that was unknown, then they were known by where they came from. Abram was "Abram son of Terah" back in Ur and Haran, but the Canaanites had never met Terah. Consequently, Abram became identified by where he came from, and this was *the other side*.

One of the things the Lord had promised Abram in Genesis 12 was that he would become a great nation. When this promise was fulfilled, the idea of "the other side" in the word Hebrew came to mean *those who are special and unique.*

To this day the Jewish people, despite the horrific amounts of anti-Semitism they have faced, possess a strong sense of identity as special and unique, and they generally have high self-esteem as individuals as well. But "the other side" must mean more than *those who are special and unique* for it to be ultimately significant. Ultimately, it must express a relationship with *the God of the other side*, the God who is on the other side of all that has been touched by sin—including limitation, lack, inability, disability, wounding, and even death.

If we belong to the God of the other side, it does not matter where we were born or who our parents were or what we experienced in the past—or even what we may be facing in the present. Conversely, if we do not belong to this God, nothing else matters.

READ: John 10
REFLECT: Psalm 100:3
PRAY: Think of all that should disqualify you from being "of God" and thank Him for choosing you anyway.

Day 63

LIVING AS ALIENS

Today we know that Abraham's alien status had spiritual significance, not least because it reflected his great faith. As we are told in the Bible's faith chapter,

> By faith he dwelt in the land of promise as in a foreign country, dwelling in tents with Isaac and Jacob, the heirs with him of the same promise; for he waited for the city which has foundations, whose builder and maker is God. (Heb. 11:9-10)

Like the patriarchs, we are to dwell in this world *as in a foreign country*, because as citizens of the kingdom of God, this world *is* a foreign country. Its systems and values are contrary to those of the kingdom of God. Whether we live in the place where we were born and raised or in a country or culture that is foreign to us, we are to live in this world as "aliens and strangers" (1 Pet. 2:11). Wherever we reside, we are to live as citizens of the kingdom of God—*in* the world but not *of* the world.

An alien does not have the same rights as a citizen. Before I became a US citizen I could not vote or hold an American passport. In the same way, as aliens in this world, we do not have the same rights as its citizens. The world's citizens have the right to assert themselves, avenge themselves, indulge themselves, and exalt themselves. They may live as they please because the world grants its citizens the right to what Hebrews 11:25 calls "the fleeting pleasures of sin."

Not so with us. As citizens of the kingdom of God, the world's rights are denied to us. We are no longer under the dominion of the world but under that of the King who said that His kingdom is "not of this world" (John 18:36), and who laid down not only His rights but His very *life*. By the cross of Christ "the world has been crucified to [us], and [we] to the world" (Gal. 6:14), and now "friendship with the world is enmity with God" (James 4:4).

By the same token, we have all the rights of the kingdom of God! As its citizens we have access to the Father through Christ (Eph. 2:18), by whose blood our sins have been forgiven (Eph. 1:7). We have the indwelling Holy Spirit to teach, counsel, correct, comfort, and guide us (John 16:13), and we have the Word of God to equip us (2 Tim. 3:16–17). We have authority "over all the power of the enemy" (Luke 10:19), as well as the grace to resist temptation (1 Cor. 10:13). As members of Christ's body, we share in "the power of His resurrection, and the fellowship of His sufferings" (Phil. 3:10), and we get to participate in the Great Commission (Matt. 28:18–20). And apart from everything we enjoy on earth, we will spend eternity in heaven. Only a fool would reject these privileges for the fleeting pleasures of sin.

READ: John 11
REFLECT: Mark 8:36
PRAY: Pick one privilege listed in the last paragraph and ask the Lord to show you how to enjoy it today.

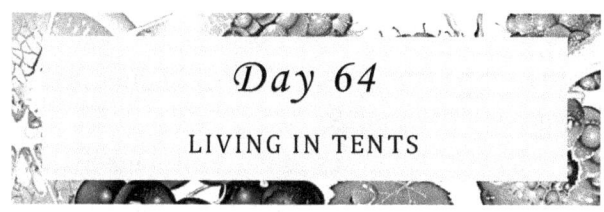

Day 64

LIVING IN TENTS

The tents in which Abraham, Isaac, and Jacob dwelt are a perfect metaphor for how we are to live as we wait for the city with foundations, whose builder and architect is God. Just as tents are a temporary structure, easy to set up and dismantle, we are to live wholly at God's disposal. This does not mean that we are to avoid making commitments or putting down roots. It means that we must daily make ourselves available to God, to be used for His purposes and not our own.

Living in tents means recognizing that this world in all its forms is passing away (1 John 2:17), and that we cannot put our hope in the things of this world. What's more, we cannot put our hope even in our own body, which itself is merely a tent.

The church's two greatest apostles both call the body a tent. Peter refers to his body as the tent he will soon put away (2 Pet. 1:14); and Paul says, "If the earthly tent we live in is destroyed, we have a building from God, an eternal house in heaven" (2 Cor. 5:1 NIV).

The word translated "tent" in 2 Peter 1:14 is *skenoma*, which conjures the image of the body as a tenement for the soul. A tenement is an apartment or room leased to a tenant, implying that our body is something we do not own. God has leased it to us for a period, and one day that lease will expire. Our body is also a tenement in that Jesus has paid the price for us and therefore we belong to Him: as Paul says, "You are not your own; you were bought at a price" (1 Cor. 6:19–20).

Skenos, the word Paul uses in 2 Corinthians 5:1, also means tabernacle, but in the sense of a hut or makeshift shelter. The word is drawn from the imagery of the Feast of Tabernacles, during which the Israelites would spend a week in booths to recall the temporary, fragile dwellings their ancestors had in the wilderness. Those ancient dwellings aptly depict our mortal bodies.

Knowing that we inhabit a temporary tent, a body that will eventually return to dust, is extremely liberating. It frees us from the obsessions and attachments that bind people who lack this assurance. And we are encouraged to live for eternity because, as Paul reminds us, "We must all appear before the judgment seat of Christ, so that each of us may receive what is due us for the things done while in the body, whether good or bad" (2 Cor. 5:10 NIV).

When we live for eternity, everything about our temporal existence gets placed in proper perspective—including our trials. Living for eternity enables us to endure suffering joyfully, knowing that our light and momentary afflictions are achieving for us "a far more exceeding and eternal weight of glory" (2 Cor. 4:17 KJV).

> *READ: John 12*
> *REFLECT: 2 Corinthians 4:17–18*
> *PRAY: Think of one of your trials and ask the Lord to use it to produce an "eternal weight of glory" for you.*

Day 65

RECEIVING OUR IDENTITY

When Melchizedek says "Blessed be Abram of God Most High," he is giving Abram an assurance of his true identity. It is significant that this happens *before* his name is changed to Abraham to reflect his destiny. Before he can inherit what God has promised, Abram must know that he belongs to God Most High, because the "destiny blessing" cannot be given outside of a relationship with God.

Abram had a close relationship with God long before the Valley of Shaveh, but it is in the King's Valley, after he has faced and defeated a deadly enemy, that Abram's identity is publicly confirmed by the priest-king Melchizedek. And since Melchizedek is a type of Christ Himself, it suggests that we must likewise receive our identity from Jesus before we can receive our destiny blessings. For Abraham that blessing was Isaac, the son through whom he would become a great nation. In our case, it's the specific things God has for us that will move us from barrenness to fruitfulness.

Our true identity is who God says we are, and we can find this throughout Scripture, from Genesis to Revelation. The words of our Lord in the Gospels and what the epistles say are especially packed with the truth about our identity. For example, whenever Jesus says "your Father," He is talking about our identity as children of the heavenly Father. And Paul is saying something similar whenever he uses his favorite terms, "in Christ," "in Him," and "in whom."

Who we are in Christ is our eternal identity; it's what we will be *forever*. When we have our eternal identity established, we won't need to wear the world's labels. The world says we are what we have, and what we look like, and what we know, and what we do. If we fall short in any of these areas, the world labels us a loser, which undermines our self-worth. Negative messages about our identity also attack our need to be loved and accepted.

Conversely, the world may send us positive messages based on our possessions and performance, but they are positive only as long as the possessions last and the performance holds up. Therefore, positive or negative, the world's labels are false and faulty sources of identity, like the foundation of sand in the parable that concludes the Sermon on the Mount (Matt. 7:26–27). Our real identity, the solid foundation upon which our lives should be built, comes from whether or not we are related to God, from whether or not we are *of God*.

When we receive the gift of salvation, all things become ours (1 Cor. 3:21), and we become "joint heirs with Christ" (Rom. 8:17). But as long as we see ourselves through the distorted lens of beliefs that don't line up with the truth, we will not be able to inherit God's promises.

READ: John 13
REFLECT: Romans 8:15
PRAY: Ask the Lord to show you where you have sought your identity apart from Him and ask His forgiveness.

Day 66

RECEIVING OUR DESTINY

In Genesis 14:19 we have the first mention of the terms "God Most High" and "Possessor of heaven and earth." Melchizedek is telling Abram that since God is the Possessor *of heaven and earth*, and since he is Abram *of God*, he can rest assured that God *will* provide for all his needs. Abram would not have received God's promises had he not known God as the Possessor of heaven and earth, for only the One who owns everything could fulfill the kind of lavish promises God made to Abram.

Our insecurity stems from the fact that we fail to see God as the Possessor of heaven and earth. If we did, we would be more confident in His ability to provide for us—not just materially but also in terms of openings and opportunities.

Too often we try to make things happen for ourselves or look to other people to open doors for us, whereas history's wisest man has said that *unless the Lord builds a house*, "they labor in vain who build it" (Ps. 127:1). As a master builder, who constructed not only cities and gardens but also the Temple of Jerusalem, Solomon knew what he was talking about.

The prophet Jeremiah has also issued a warning to the one who trusts in man: such a person "will not see prosperity when it comes. Instead, they will dwell in the parched places of the desert, in a salt land where no one lives" (Jer. 17:6 NIV).

The Hebrew word for a salt land or desert, *melachah*, is the same word for barrenness. By contrast, this is what Jeremiah tells those who trust in the Lord:

> Blessed is the one who trusts in the LORD, whose confidence is in the LORD. They will be like a tree planted by the water, that sends out its roots by the stream. It does not fear when heat comes; its leaves are always green. It . . . never fails to bear fruit. (Jer. 17:7–8 NIV)

Each of us has a special and unique destiny. None of us is an accident, and God has planted His dreams for our lives within us all. As He famously says, "I know the plans I have for you, declares the LORD, plans to prosper you and not to harm you, plans to give you hope and a future" (Jer. 29:11 NIV). And Paul later affirms, "Eye has not seen, nor ear heard, Nor have entered into the heart of man The things which God has prepared for those who love Him" (1 Cor. 2:9).

We are "God's handiwork, created in Christ Jesus to do good works, which God prepared in advance for us to do" (Eph. 2:10 NIV). We can certainly fulfill many of our own dreams apart from God, but we will never fulfill *God's* dreams for us unless we know Him in a relationship of faith and obedience. And while our own dreams may result in works that outlast our lifetime, only *God's* dreams produce works that will endure throughout eternity, what Jesus refers to as "fruit that will last" (John 15:16 NIV).

READ: John 14
REFLECT: 1 Corinthians 2:9
PRAY: Thank the Lord for His plans for you and ask Him to help you trust Him more today.

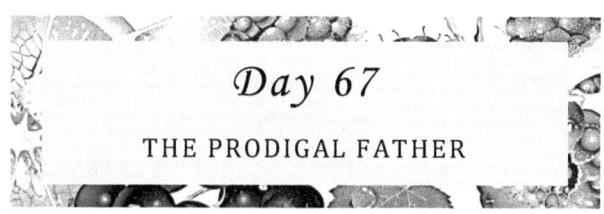

Day 67

THE PRODIGAL FATHER

Terah may have had an inkling of his firstborn's destiny when he named him Abram, but Terah's knowledge was partial. Only the heavenly Father could reveal to Abram the full extent of his destiny, and that was to be *Abraham*.

A significant aspect of Abraham's destiny is to reflect God the Father. The event in which this is most clearly manifested is the binding of Isaac, but God's fatherhood is also revealed in each of Abraham's names. Abram means *exalted father*, which God Himself is, and Abraham means *father of many nations*, which God also is. Although He is the Creator and King of the universe, God is first and foremost a Father. This may be why the first word in the Hebrew dictionary is *ab* or *father*.

"Father" is the term Jesus used most frequently when referring to God. His teaching, His prayers, and His work on the cross all demonstrated that God is our Father. And in His final words before ascending into heaven, Jesus spoke of the Holy Spirit as "the Promise of the Father" (Luke 24:49).

The poignant parable titled "The Prodigal Son" is in fact about a prodigal *father*, whose love is prodigal to the point of folly. He gives the boy his portion of the inheritance even though it was to be obtained upon his own death; and he gives it knowing that the boy might leave home and squander the money—and of course the boy does just that. When the money is gone, he comes to his senses and decides to return to his father, to beg forgiveness and apply for a servant's job. *But while he is yet a long way off*, his father sees him and runs to him and falls on his neck and smothers him with kisses.

"Father, I have sinned against heaven and against you," says the boy. "I am no longer worthy to be called your son."

He does not get to apply for the servant's job, for the apology has no sooner left his lips than the father sets about proving that the son is still very much a son. He orders the servants to bring out the best robe, a ring, and sandals—all marks of sonship in that culture—and to kill the fatted calf in celebration. And to forever settle the issue of whether the boy is worthy to be called his son, the father refers to him as *"this my son"* (Luke 15:24).

Like the other two parables in Luke 15, this one is about God, who seeks and saves the lost. The lengths to which the shepherd and the woman go to search for their lost sheep and coin, and the extravagant welcome the father gives his repentant son, should leave us in no doubt as to our heavenly Father's relentless love, and His readiness to forgive us and give us the special blessings reserved for His children.

All who believe in Jesus are given "the right to become children of God, who were born, not of . . . the will of man, but of God" (John 1:12-13 ESV). God has so lavished His love upon us that we can be called His sons and daughters—and as 1 John 3:1 declares, *that is what we are!*

> READ: John 15
> REFLECT: Matthew 6:9
> PRAY: *Thank your heavenly Father for His love and forgive your earthly father if he failed to love you unconditionally.*

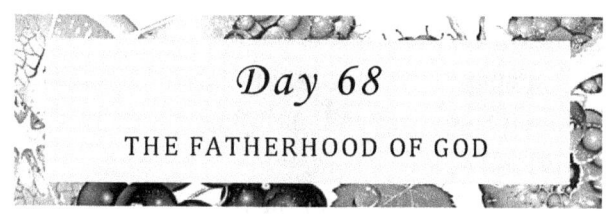

Day 68

THE FATHERHOOD OF GOD

The fatherhood of God is rooted in His character. Father is not a role God plays; it's who He *is*. And who He is can be summed up in one word: *good*.

When Moses asked the Lord to show him His glory, God said, "I will make all My *goodness* pass before you" (Ex. 33:19). In other words, *God's glory is His goodness*. And He is good both in His character and in His deeds. As the psalmist declares, "You are good, and what you do is good" (Ps. 119:68 NIV).

On that momentous occasion when Moses sees the Lord, he is standing in a cleft on Mount Sinai. In a scene almost impossible to imagine, the Lord descends in a cloud and passes by in front of Moses proclaiming His name and His character:

> The LORD, the LORD, the compassionate and gracious God, slow to anger, abounding in love and faithfulness, maintaining love to thousands, and forgiving wickedness, rebellion and sin. Yet he does not leave the guilty unpunished. (Ex. 34:6–7 NIV)

Thus the Lord reveals Himself to be compassionate, gracious, patient, loving, faithful, forgiving, and just. These seven qualities are captured in the Hebrew word *hesed*. Typically translated lovingkindness, unfailing love, and goodness, *hesed* is a covenantal commitment for the well-being of another, a commitment marked by mercy and compassion. It is much more than a feeling of goodwill, for it is displayed primarily through its *actions*, as the parable of the Good Samaritan in Luke 10 teaches. The Greek equivalent for this kind of love is *agape*.

Hesed is the overall theme of the psalms. When the psalmists speak of God's *hesed*, they are referring to the covenantal manner in which He relates with His creation, and that is inseparable from who He is. He rescues, redeems, restores, and responds to us out of the goodness of His very *being*. We learn from the psalms that God's lovingkindness is vast, unending, and even "better than life" (Ps. 63:4).

The first instance of *hesed* in the Bible appears in the context of the destruction of Sodom and Gomorrah. These cities have invited judgment upon themselves, but Lot finds mercy because of God's *hesed* (Gen. 19:19). The incident is a disturbing one, but it is ultimately encouraging because it shows us both aspects of God's goodness at once: His justice and His mercy.

Often when people are suffering—or even when they are only pondering the problem of pain—they find satisfactory answers that are not directly related to God. These answers offer a measure of comfort and the wherewithal to carry on, but they are at best only temporal, like the temporary palliatives mentioned on Day 41. The most effective of them will last only as long as this life does. Our quest for answers that transcend this world must lead us to the essence of God, and that is His goodness.

> READ: *John 16*
> REFLECT: *Psalm 136:1*
> PRAY: *Ask the Holy Spirit to give you a fresh revelation of one quality God lists in Exodus 34:6–7.*

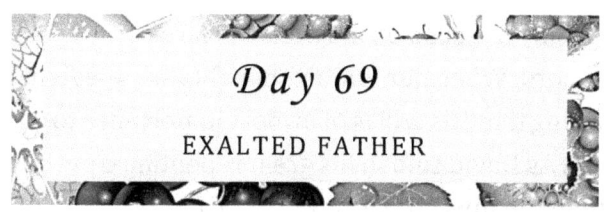

Day 69

EXALTED FATHER

As we have already seen, the name Abram means *exalted father*. The Hebrew word for exalted, *rum*, means to be high or raised, like a hill or a throne. Our English verb exalt is derived from the Latin *exaltare*, meaning to lift up, and this is how we are to lift up or elevate God: "Glorify the Lord in your body and in your spirit" (1 Cor. 6:20). What this verse is saying is that we must exalt the Lord with our lives ("in your body") and with our worship ("in your spirit").

We exalt the Lord with our lives by giving Him first place in all things, be it our time, our talents, our resources, or our affections. How we handle suffering, temptation, and the mundane things can also exalt the Lord, if we do so with faith, patience, and obedience. Christ must have preeminence in *all things* (Col. 1:18).

Three times in Matthew 6 Jesus says that our Father "sees what is done in secret" (vv. 4,6,18), which implies that our private life must glorify the Lord. As Paul exhorts,

> Whatever is true, whatever is noble, whatever is right, whatever is pure, whatever is pure, whatever is lovely, whatever is admirable—if anything is excellent or praiseworthy—think about such things. (Phil. 4:8 NIV)

As noted on Day 12, Paul tells us that we are to bring "every thought into captivity to the obedience of Christ" (2 Cor. 10:5). But this is not only a means of spiritual warfare. It also counts as exalting the Lord. When our inmost thoughts are obedient to Christ, we are saying that His will is of utmost importance to us, and that exalts Him. As David said in his great repentance psalm, "You desire truth in the inward parts" (Ps. 51:6).

Naturally, our public deeds must also glorify the Father. As Jesus has said, "Let your light shine before men in such a way that they may see your good works, and glorify your Father who is in heaven" (Matt. 5:16 NASB).

The second way we exalt the Lord—with our worship—is primarily an attitude of the heart and spirit. Nevertheless, we must also elevate the Lord by declaring our praises in speech and song. The psalmists have much to say on this, and it can be summarized in a cry of David's that appears twice in Psalm 57: "Be exalted, O God, above the heavens; Let Your glory be above all the earth" (vv. 5,11).

Psalm 57 was composed in a cave where David was hiding from Saul, and it is an excellent example of what happens when we exalt the Lord. In the first part of the psalm David is focused on his perilous plight, but something shifts when he exalts the Lord. Suddenly his heart becomes steadfast and he begins to sing and give praise. By the end, he is even talking about praising the Lord among the nations!

READ: *John 17*
REFLECT: *Isaiah 25:1*
PRAY: *Ask the Lord to show you one way you can exalt Him today and pray for the grace to do so.*

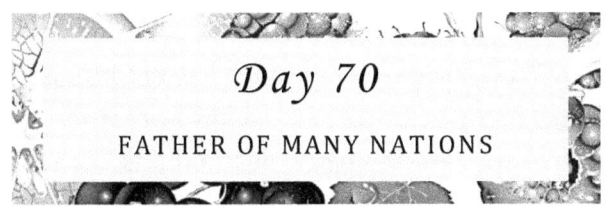

Day 70
FATHER OF MANY NATIONS

When Abram is ninety-nine and still living in his tent by the oaks of Mamre, God appears to him and says, "No longer shall your name be called Abram, but your name shall be Abraham: for I have made you a father of many nations" (Gen. 17:5). A key phrase in this verse is "*I have made you.*" It suggests that becoming fitted for our destiny is a work of God: *He* is the one who makes or forms us into the people who will inherit His promises.

The perfect tense of the verb ("I *have made* you") also tells us that God's plans for us originate in His heart long before it's time to reveal them to us. Ephesians 2:10 speaks of the good works God has prepared *in advance* for us to do. Long before we were born again, long before we were even *born*, our Father had good things planned for us. He tells Abraham "I have made you a father of many nations" well before the son of promise is anywhere in the picture—*such* is the faith of God! *Such* is God's confidence in His ability to do what He has promised.

The names Abram and Abraham are very similar; the difference is only the addition of one small syllable—but it's an all-important syllable. The syllable added to make Abram Abraham is the fifth letter of the Hebrew alphabet—*heh*—and on Day 2 we noted that in the Bible the number five represents grace. Since grace is unmerited favor, the new syllable reiterates the truth that being fitted for our destiny is a work of God. We cannot claim any credit for it. Though we are required to live in continual faith and obedience, even the grace to do so comes from Him.

Abraham had many biological descendants, but his true children are his spiritual heirs. John the Baptist warned the Pharisees and the Sadducees that unless their lives reflected true repentance, they could not claim to have Abraham as their father (Matt. 3:8-9). And Jesus Himself told the Jews,

> I know that you are Abraham's *descendants*, but you seek to kill Me, because My word has no place in you.... If you were Abraham's *children*, you would do the works of Abraham. (John 8:37,39)

The distinction between *descendants* and *children* must be noted, for biological descent does not guarantee spiritual inheritance. As Paul will say, "Only those who are of faith are sons of Abraham" (Gal. 3:7).

We become Abraham's sons or spiritual heirs by giving Jesus' word first place in our lives and by doing the works of Abraham. Abraham's works were faith and obedience; and since he is the father of all who believe, faith and obedience must be the works of his children.

READ: *John 18*
REFLECT: *Galatians 3:7-9*
PRAY: *Pick two nations—your own and one other—and exalt the Lord over those nations.*

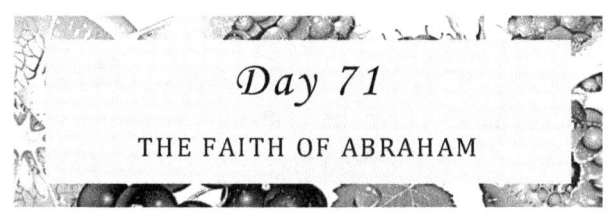

Day 71

THE FAITH OF ABRAHAM

The New Testament chapter in which we learn most about Abraham's defining trait is not Hebrews 11 but Romans 4, where he is called the father of all who believe. Paul lists seven qualities of Abraham's faith in this chapter, which we will study over the next seven days.

First, Abraham had faith while he was "still uncircumcised" (Rom. 4:11). He was not a Jew but *an uncircumcised Gentile* when he believed in God's word and it was "credited to him as righteousness" (Gen. 15:6 NIV). Therefore, belonging to the faith of Abraham is irrespective of whether one is born Jewish or Gentile.

The physical circumcision that God later commanded Abraham, as "a sign of the covenant between Me and you" (Gen. 17:11), works at the metaphorical and typological levels as well. It is symbolic of repentance and wholehearted obedience, which is required of all God's people, not just Jewish males. In his farewell address, Moses himself says,

> Now, Israel, what does the LORD your God require from you but to fear the LORD your God, to walk in all His ways and love Him, and to serve the LORD your God with all your heart and with all your soul, and to keep the LORD's commandments and His statutes which I am commanding you today for your good? . . . *So circumcise your heart.* (Deut. 10:12–13,16 NASB)

At the end, just before he blesses the twelve tribes, Moses adds, "The LORD your God will circumcise your heart and the heart of your descendants, to love the LORD your God with all your heart and with all your soul, that you may live" (Deut. 30:6). As it turns out, Israel frequently disobeys the command to love the Lord with all their heart, and centuries later Jeremiah will again remind the people of Judah to circumcise themselves and their hearts to the Lord (Jer. 4:4).

Typologically, circumcision foreshadowed the spiritual surgery God's Spirit would perform on the heart under the new covenant, where "circumcision is that of the heart, in the Spirit" (Rom. 2:29). The Spirit's work of transforming a person inwardly applies to all who are in Christ—Jew or Gentile, slave or free, male or female (Gal. 3:28).

This inner circumcision, visible not in the flesh but in a transformed life, indicates that we are the seed of Abraham and that our faith, like his, is also apart from outward circumcision. As Paul asserts, "Circumcision is nothing and uncircumcision is nothing. *Keeping God's commands is what counts*" (1 Cor. 7:19 NIV). And again, "In Christ Jesus neither circumcision nor uncircumcision avails anything, but *faith working through love*" (Gal. 5:6).

READ: John 19
REFLECT: Galatians 5:6
PRAY: Ask the Holy Spirit to help you display "faith working through love" in some situation today.

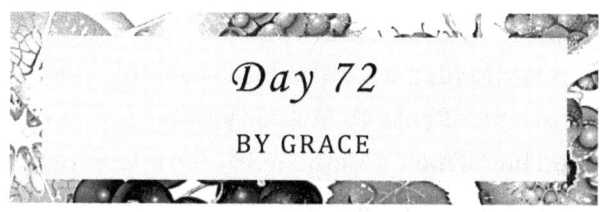

Day 72

BY GRACE

Abraham's faith was "according to grace" (Rom. 4:16). The context of this verse is imputed righteousness—the righteousness we receive from God by faith—and here grace refers to God's unmerited favor, the kindness He has extended in offering us the gift of salvation through Jesus' atoning work on the cross. As Ephesians 2:8 says, we are saved by grace through faith.

When Paul refers to "the offense of the cross" (Gal. 5:11), the Greek word *skandalon* means stumbling block or cause for error. The message of the cross is a stumbling block because it runs contrary to everything we believe, both about the Messiah and about ourselves, and it explains why many reject the free gift of salvation.

The natural human mind cannot comprehend a crucified Messiah. To such a mind, a messiah can only be a triumphant, heroic figure, not one who would allow himself to be treated as Jesus was. Crucifixion was among the most humiliating modes of execution ever devised, for which reason skeptics think Jesus died a failure. Such people clearly don't believe in the resurrection: Christ may have been "crucified in weakness," but He "lives by the power of God" (2 Cor. 13:4 ESV).

A failure is someone who fails to meet their goal, but the cross was Jesus' goal from the start. It was not thrust upon Him; He *chose* it. That's why when Peter rebuked Him for speaking of His death, Jesus responded with a counter-rebuke: "Get behind Me, Satan! You are an offense to Me, for you are not mindful of the things of God but of men" (Matt. 16:23). It's interesting that Jesus uses the same word that Paul will use of the cross—*skandalon*.

On another occasion He said, "No one takes [My life] from Me, but I lay it down of Myself. I have power to lay it down, and I have power to take it again" (John 10:18). Since Jesus is the only person in history to have done both things—lay down His life as well as rise from the dead—He is not a failure but the greatest success of all time!

Another aspect of the *skandalon* is that Jesus' work on the cross offends our flesh, which considers itself both good enough to earn its way to heaven and not bad enough to need a savior. Many reject the gospel because they simply lack the humility it takes. In the first Beatitude, when Jesus said, "Blessed are the poor in spirit, for theirs is the kingdom of heaven" (Matt. 5:3), He was referring to the attitude of humility that can admit, "My salvation will have to come from an outside source, because I am not good or powerful enough to save myself."

Being poor in spirit is the only way a person can enter the kingdom of heaven, for only the poor in spirit can accept that what Jesus did on the cross, He did for *them*. Only such a person can take an honest look at their life and say, like the apostle Paul, "By the grace of God I am what I am" (1 Cor. 15:10 NIV).

> READ: John 20
> REFLECT: John 20:29
> PRAY: Think of someone you know who is offended at the cross and pray for them to become "poor in spirit."

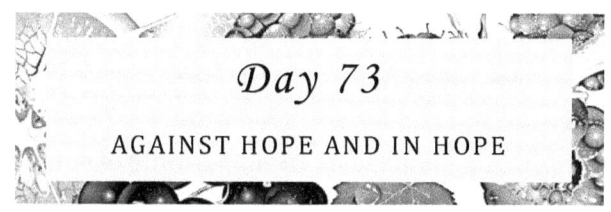

Day 73
AGAINST HOPE AND IN HOPE

Abraham's faith was *against* hope and *in* hope: "contrary to hope, in hope [he] believed" (Rom. 4:18). It was both against hope and in hope because the two hopes are not identical. The first is based on how things are going. It is dependent on circumstances, and circumstances can go well or badly. Abraham's faith was against this variable kind of hope. It was contrary to the facts, because the facts were contrary to what God had said.

The first kind of hope, the kind Abraham's faith was against, is merely optimism. It is *a feeling of hopefulness*, and feelings come and go. Even the most stable person cannot sustain one emotional state forever. Moreover, certain personality types find it easier to feel optimistic, whereas God wants *all* His children to have hope, not just those with a naturally sunny disposition or those who can pull themselves up by the mental bootstraps and *will* themselves to feel hopeful. Biblical hope is not a feeling, and it is irrespective of temperament, otherwise it would not be available equally to all.

Biblical hope is based on who God is: as Peter tells us, "Your faith and hope are *in God*" (1 Pet. 1:21). Since God never changes, hope in Him is "an anchor for the soul, both sure and steadfast" (Heb. 6:19). This hope does not go by what the facts say, because it gets its orders from a higher authority. Abraham placed his faith in this hope, and he was not disappointed: as the Lord has declared, "Those who hope in me will not be disappointed" (Is. 49:23 NIV).

The prophet Jeremiah is a classic example of someone who, despite his dismal circumstances and melancholic temperament, hoped in the Lord. In Lamentations 3, after bewailing his plight at some length, he eventually acknowledges, "Yet this I call to mind and therefore I have hope: Because of the LORD's great love we are not consumed, for his compassions never fail" (vv. 21–22 NIV). Jeremiah can have hope because of who God is: his hope is rooted in the character of God.

"Hope does not disappoint," writes Paul in Romans 5:5, "because the love of God has been poured out in our hearts by the Holy Spirit who was given to us." The hope that arises from God's love being poured into our hearts by the Holy Spirit is the hope that does not, and indeed *cannot*, disappoint.

In Romans 8:24 Paul will say, "Hope that is seen is not hope" (ESV). The Greek word repeated twice in this verse, *elpis*, meaning expectation, trust, and confidence, is derived from *elpo*, which means to anticipate or welcome. It implies the expectation of what is sure or certain and is thus virtually identical to the definition of faith in Hebrews 11:1—"the substance of things hoped for, the evidence of things not seen."

> READ: John 21
> REFLECT: Hebrews 6:19–20
> PRAY: Think of one disappointment you have faced and ask the Lord to give you His hope.

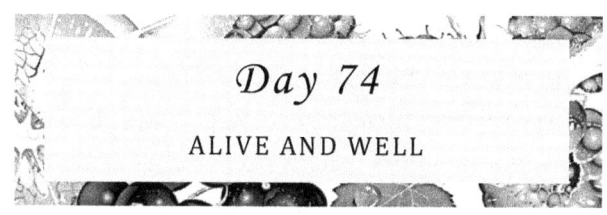

Day 74

ALIVE AND WELL

Abraham's faith was not "dead" like his own body and "the deadness of Sarah's womb" (Rom. 4:19). It was alive because it did what faith is meant to do, which is to *believe*. It was also alive because the object of his faith was the living God, who "gives life to the dead and calls those things which do not exist as though they were" (v. 17).

As we noted on Day 44, everything stands or falls on whether we believe in Christ's resurrection. Believing that our Lord vanquished death by rising again is an intrinsic part of our salvation. Paul makes this quite clear: "If you confess with your mouth the Lord Jesus and believe in your heart that God has raised Him from the dead, you will be saved" (Rom. 10:9).

One cannot hope to receive salvation or eternal life from a dead savior, which is why Paul also says that if Christ had not been raised we are still in our sins and our faith is "futile" (1 Cor. 15:17). And Peter reminds us that God has "caused us to be born again into a living hope through the resurrection of Jesus Christ from the dead, to obtain an inheritance which is imperishable" (1 Pet. 1:3–4 NASB).

Like Paul, our desire should be to "know [Christ] and the power of His resurrection" (Phil. 3:10), because the resurrection affects every area of our lives, not just our eternal destiny. Because

Jesus is alive, He can change those situations that are so hopeless they might as well be dead.

In the first raising miracle recorded in the New Testament, Jairus had a sliver of hope when he approached Jesus on behalf of his sick daughter. Her condition was critical, but she was still alive. Jesus' arrival at the house is delayed by the episode of the hemorrhaging woman, and meanwhile the girl dies. The sliver of hope also dies, and Jairus tells Jesus not to bother coming to his house. It is in this place of complete hopelessness that Jesus says, "*Do not be afraid; only believe*" (Mark 5:36). Jairus chooses to obey Jesus and lets his faith triumph over his fear, and in this he has left us a priceless legacy.

The next raising miracle is of the widow of Nain's only son (Luke 7:11–17). The widow's predicament is more hopeless yet, because she now has no one to comfort or provide for her. Jairus at least had his wife, and as ruler of the synagogue he had an income. The widow has neither—*but Jesus is walking by!* He has compassion on her and turns her weeping into rejoicing by doing something only He can do. We learn from this brief story that even truly hopeless situations can be transformed by Jesus' presence, His compassion, and His power.

And in the last raising miracle of the Gospels, just before He calls Lazarus out of the tomb, Jesus gives Martha the ultimate revelation of Himself: "I am the resurrection and the life" (John 11:25). He follows this up with a question we must all answer: "*Do you believe this?*"

> READ: Galatians 1
> REFLECT: Philippians 3:10
> PRAY: *Pray for one hopeless situation in your life or someone else's that needs the power of Christ's resurrection.*

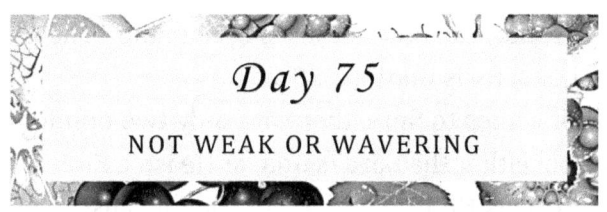

Day 75

NOT WEAK OR WAVERING

Abraham did not become "weak in faith" (Rom. 4:19). Up to this point in the New Testament, the Greek verb *astheneo* has been used only of physical weakness, such as the sickness of Lazarus in John 11:3 and Dorcas in Acts 9:37. That these disciples died as a result of their sickness suggests that weakness does to faith what sickness did to Lazarus and Dorcas. Thankfully, our spiritual father did not allow his faith to become weak and die.

Furthermore, although both he and Sarah were past childbearing, Abraham "did not waver at the promise of God" (Rom. 4:20). The verb *diakrino* literally means to judge back and forth. Like its English counterpart discriminate, *diakrino* can be used in a positive or a negative sense.

To waver at God's promise is to vacillate between thinking that He will fulfill it and that He won't. This is unbelief, not faith! As noted on Day 6, the Hebrew word translated faith, *emunah*, means firmness and steadfastness. To have faith is to steadfastly hold on to God's promises because we trust His character.

Unbelief causes us to waver, a word Elijah famously used before his epic showdown with the prophets of Baal on Mount Carmel. "How long will you waver between two opinions?" Elijah tells the Israelites. "If the LORD is God, follow him" (1 Kings 18:21 NIV). The people say nothing at the time, but when the Lord answers by fire, they fall on their faces exclaiming, "The LORD, He is God! The LORD, He is God!" (v. 39).

When it comes to faith, there are only two opinions we waver between: either the Lord is God, or He isn't. Either God is everything He says He is, or He is not. Doubt causes us to waver between these two opinions, and things that waver are not steady. In spiritual terms, what wavers cannot be established: as Isaiah had told King Ahaz, "If you will not believe, surely you will not be established" (Is. 7:9). By the same token, if we *will* believe, surely we *will* be established.

One of the strongest warnings against wavering comes from James the brother of the Lord:

> If any of you lacks wisdom, you should ask God.... But when you ask, you must believe and not doubt, because *the one who doubts is like a wave of the sea*, blown and tossed by the wind. That person should not expect to receive anything from the Lord. Such a person is *double-minded and unstable in all they do*. (James 1:5–8 NIV)

The immediate context of these words is asking God for wisdom; but as verse 4 suggests, we must believe without doubting when we ask God for *anything* that will keep us from being mature and complete. And as James goes on to say in verse 17, every good and perfect gift comes from the Father, who Himself does not change or waver.

READ: Galatians 2
REFLECT: James 1:6–8
PRAY: Ask the Lord to show you an area where you have been doubleminded and receive His grace to change.

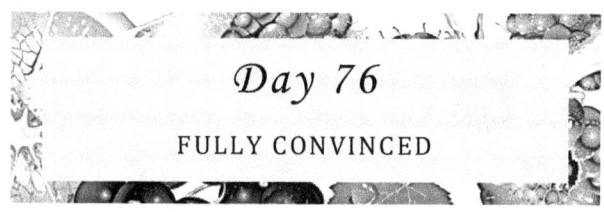

Day 76

FULLY CONVINCED

Abraham was "fully convinced" with regard to God's promise (Rom. 4:21). He was convinced that God would do what He had said—and convinced to the *full* extent. The Greek word used in this verse, *plerophoreo*, means to be fully persuaded, to fully carry through, and to bear (or wear) fully. Two of Abraham's descendants who exemplify this quality of being fully convinced are Joshua and Caleb.

When Moses sends the twelve spies to spy out the land of Canaan, they return forty days later with two conflicting reports. Ten bring a report that is based on their lack of faith, and it incites the people to panic and rebel. Joshua and Caleb are the only two with a report that is based on faith. They say the land "flows with milk and honey," and they urge the Israelites, "Do not rebel against the LORD, nor fear the people of the land, for they are our bread; . . . and the LORD is with us" (Num. 14:8–9).

Since God is on their side, Joshua and Caleb believe that defeating the inhabitants of Canaan will be as easy as gobbling down bread. But the unbelief of the other ten spies has infected the people, and they talk about stoning Moses and Aaron and picking a new leader to take them back to Egypt.

The incident has three serious consequences. The unbelieving spies are immediately killed by a plague. The Israelites will now have to wander in the wilderness for forty years, one year for each day the spies had spent in Canaan. And Joshua and Caleb will be *the only two people* over twenty who are allowed to enter the Promised Land.

The writer of Hebrews, when cautioning us against "a sinful, unbelieving heart that turns away from the living God" (Heb. 3:12 NIV), reminds us that the rest of that generation could not enter the land because they "believed not" (v. 18 KJV). The Greek word *apeitheo* refers to an inward refusal to be persuaded, which is outwardly manifested in disobedience. Its opposite, *peitheo*, means to allow oneself to be persuaded of what is trustworthy. Thus, both unbelief and belief involve an act of the will.

The Israelites' refusal to obey God in the desert is also mentioned in the great prayer made by the Levites after the Babylonian exiles return to Jerusalem (Neh. 9:5–38). But the first person named in that prayer is Abraham, and the Levites pay him this rich tribute: *"You found his heart faithful before You"* (v. 8). Based on what we know of Abraham, the word faithful applies in both senses—loyal and full of faith.

The hortative sections of Hebrews, interspersed throughout the epistle, were written to encourage readers not to slip into unbelief and disobedience. If these sins cost a generation of Israelites the Promised Land, they will likewise cause us not to inherit God's promises, which are contingent upon our walking in faith and obedience like Abraham, the man of faith.

READ: Galatians 3
REFLECT: Hebrews 3:12
PRAY: Think of a promise Jesus makes in the Gospels and ask the Holy Spirit to help you be fully convinced about it.

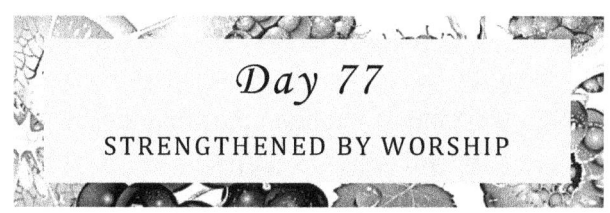

Day 77
STRENGTHENED BY WORSHIP

Finally, Abraham's faith was strengthened by "giving glory to God" (Rom. 4:20). This phrase is synonymous with worship, which involves *praising God* for who He is and *thanking Him* for what He has done, as we know from Psalm 100:4. Since faith sees what is unseen, people of faith also thank God for what He *will* do and praise Him when circumstances are difficult.

The word worship is derived from the Old English *weorthscipe*, which referred to the acknowledgement of worth or worthiness. Thus, to worship someone is to ascribe worth to them, and only God is that worthy. Some of the Hebrew words that are translated worship include *shachah*, meaning to bow down, to do obeisance, and to humbly beseech; *darash*, meaning to seek; and *yare*, meaning to fear.

One of the most powerful examples in the Bible of how worship strengthens God's people is the episode recorded in 2 Chronicles 20. When King Jehoshaphat learns that the Moabites and Ammonites are advancing, he proclaims a fast throughout the kingdom of Judah, and the people assemble to seek the Lord. Next morning Jehoshaphat appoints worshipers to sing praises to the Lord as the army marches into battle, and the enemies are routed. It takes the king and his people a good three days to haul away the spoils of war! On the fourth day they gather in the Valley of

Berakah, meaning *blessing*, where they praise God for blessing them with victory.

In the New Testament we have that memorable incident in Acts 16, where Paul and Silas worship God in the Philippian jail. Praise causes their chains to fall off, and the jailor and his entire household are saved as a result. No doubt these people shared their faith with others, and those others with yet others. We will find out only in eternity how many lives were touched because Paul and Silas praised God that night.

Worship is one of the most effective means of engaging in spiritual warfare, which is why we must be prepared to face resistance when we resolve to worship God. The devil knows that our faith is strengthened by worship, and he wants us to stay weak and ineffective.

The devil also hates us worshipping God because that was his role in heaven, before he became filled with pride and led a rebellion against God. Now he covets worship so much that he even offered Jesus the kingdoms of the world in exchange for worship (Matt. 4:8–9). But the Son of God refused to wrongfully acquire His inheritance and instead went on to obtain it rightfully, by paying for it with His own blood.

The more we meditate on this immense sacrifice, the more will we be stirred to worship Jesus. One day every tongue will confess that He is Lord, "to the glory of God the Father" (Phil. 2:11), and blessed are those who begin *here and now*.

> *READ: Galatians 4*
> *REFLECT: Ephesians 5:20*
> *PRAY: Praise God for one of His attributes and thank Him for something He has done for you recently.*

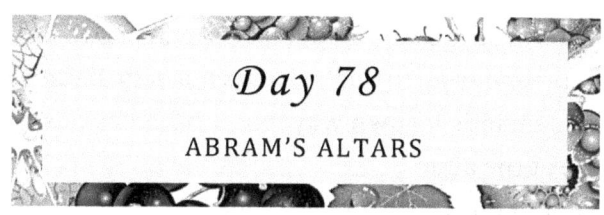

Day 78

ABRAM'S ALTARS

We have much to learn from Abraham's rich devotional life. In particular, the four times we see him at an altar before he meets Melchizedek teach us how to prepare for blessing.

The word altar derives from the Latin *altare* meaning elevated, but the Hebrew *mizbeach* refers to a place of slaughter or sacrifice. Although an atoning sacrifice is no longer required, since Christ our Passover was sacrificed for us (1 Cor. 5:7), we still need to offer the sacrifice of our *self*. This is aptly described by Paul in terms of crucifixion: "Those who belong to Christ Jesus have *crucified the flesh* with its passions and desires" (Gal. 5:24 NIV). And when writing to the Romans, he says:

> Our old self was crucified with [Jesus]. . . . Count yourselves dead to sin but alive to God in Christ Jesus. . . . Offer every part of yourself to [God] as an instrument of righteousness. (Rom. 6:6,11,13 NIV)

These verses recall Jesus' own words in the Gospels, where He had spoken about discipleship in terms of taking up one's cross. He said: "Whoever wants to be my disciple must deny themselves and *take up their cross* and follow me" (Matt. 16:24 NIV). And: "Whoever does not *carry their cross* and follow me cannot be my disciple" (Luke 14:27 NIV). Thus, according to Jesus Himself, the essential element in following Him is *self-denial*.

As the term suggests, self-denial is saying no to our own desires and surrendering to God's. This is not easy, because the carnal nature demands its own way; but it becomes possible as we spend time at the altar.

The altar of our heart is the place where we give God all that we have to offer—our weaknesses, wounds, and sins as well as our love, worship, and thanksgiving. We acknowledge God's sole ownership of our lives and present our bodies as "a living sacrifice, holy and acceptable to God," for that is our "spiritual worship" (Rom. 12:1 ESV). At the altar we enthrone Christ and dethrone ourselves, where we declare, like John the Baptist, "He must increase, but I must decrease" (John 3:30 NASB).

When God gave Moses His first instructions about the altar He said, "In every place where I record My name, *I will come to you and I will bless you*" (Ex. 20:24). The Lord longs to come near us and bless us, but He can only do so *in the place where He can record His name*. In other words, where His

While it's helpful to have the same quiet spot for our daily devotions, what matters most is our *internal* state, the condition of our spirit, because *that's* the place where we worship God: as Jesus told the Samaritan woman, "True worshipers will worship the Father *in spirit and truth*" (John 4:23). This is why Abraham could keep moving and still maintain a consistent devotional life. His real altar was his heart.

READ: Galatians 5
REFLECT: John 4:23
PRAY: Ask the Lord to help you deny yourself in some situation today when you'd rather gratify your flesh.

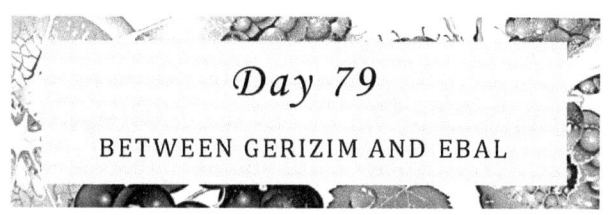

Day 79
BETWEEN GERIZIM AND EBAL

After Abram leaves Haran and reaches the land of Canaan, the Lord appears to him at Shechem and says, "To your descendants I will give this land" (Gen. 12:7). Abram responds by building an altar to the Lord.

Shechem was a fortified city at the intersection of certain major highways and trade routes. Its location, between the barren Mount Ebal and the fertile Mount Gerizim, was symbolic. Centuries later Moses, in his farewell speech, instructed the Israelites to reserve Gerizim for the blessing and Ebal for the curse (Deut. 11:29). When they entered the Promised Land, six tribes were to proclaim the blessing from Mount Gerizim, and six the curse from Mount Ebal (Deut. 27:12–13). Shechem, situated between these two mountains, was thus within the sound of both the blessings of following God and the curses of forsaking Him. This midway location of Abram's first altar suggests that it is up to a person to decide whether they want to live under the blessing or the curse.

After the tribes take possession of Canaan, Joshua assembles them at Shechem and says:

> Choose for yourselves this day whom you will serve, whether the gods your ancestors served beyond the Euphrates, or the gods of the Amorites, in whose land you are living. But as for me and my household, we will serve the Lord. (Josh. 24:15 NIV)

Joshua is no doubt referring to Terah's idols when he says "the gods your ancestors served beyond the Euphrates." Terah was the last ancestor to live beyond the Euphrates, since Abram had to cross the river when God called him out of Haran.

An idol is anything that a person looks to for blessing, meaning, comfort, power, and life. Since these gifts are to come from God, when a person seeks them from an idol, they are effectively saying, "This is my God." And whether one uses the word worship or not, by turning to it for what God alone can give, they are in fact worshipping it.

Terah's gods were probably carvings and statues, but idols can take many forms. They typically include money, material possessions, bodily pleasures, people, work, hobbies, and talents. Intangible things like beliefs, ideologies, status, reputation, ambitions, and dreams also count as idols.

In Ezekiel 14:3 God speaks of those who have "set up their idols in their hearts, and put before them that which causes them to stumble into iniquity." This verse tells us two critical things about idolatry.

First, it's *an issue of the heart*. Our heart is where we enthrone either God or idols. Second, it *causes us to stumble into sin*. As a violation of the first commandment (Ex. 20:2), idolatry of any kind is a sin; but according to Ezekiel 14:3 it also *leads to* sin. In other words, unrighteousness begets unrighteousness.

READ: Galatians 6
REFLECT: Exodus 20:3
PRAY: Ask the Lord which of the idols listed He wants you to forsake, and receive His grace to forsake it today.

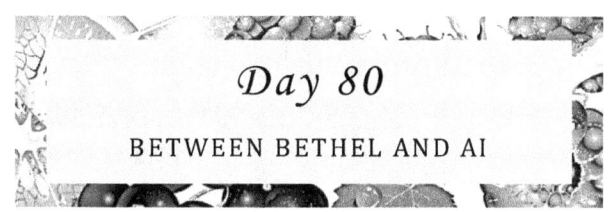

Day 80

BETWEEN BETHEL AND AI

Since Abram is leading the nomadic life of a foreigner, he has to keep moving. He leaves Shechem and pitches his tent between Bethel and Ai, and once again he builds an altar. On this occasion we are also told that Abram "called on the name of the LORD" (Gen. 12:8), which suggests that his relationship with the Lord is becoming stronger and more established.

A person can only call on the name of the Lord when they *know* the name of the Lord—and by "know" we mean a personal, experiential knowledge that touches the heart and transforms the life, not technical, theoretical knowledge that remains in the realm of the intellect.

The Hebrew verb *qara* in Genesis 12:8 means both *cry unto* and *address*. We first read of people calling upon the name of the Lord during the time of Seth (Gen. 4:26). Scripture teaches us to call on the Lord in time of need as well as in worship. Need is often what drives people to God for the first time, but we cannot consistently call upon His name unless we know it relationally and personally. As David has said, "Those who *know Your name* will trust in You" (Ps. 9:10).

The location of Abram's second altar is as significant as the first. Bethel means *house of God* and Ai means *ruin*, which suggests that we must worship the Lord wherever we are—in places where we can experience a palpable sense of God's presence, as well as in places that are ruined by sin. We are to call on the name of the Lord when we are among other believers and when we are amid people who not only don't believe in God but who also persecute those who do.

In Genesis 12:8 we have the first mention of Bethel and Ai, both of which are more commonly associated with other men. Bethel is better known as the place where Jacob dreamt of the ladder reaching up to heaven, with angels ascending and descending on it. There the Lord tells Jacob,

> I am the LORD God of Abraham your father and the God of Isaac; the land on which you lie I will give to you and your descendants.... In you and in your seed all the families of the earth shall be blessed. Behold, I am with you and will keep you wherever you go, and will bring you back to this land; for I will not leave you until I have done what I have spoken to you. (Gen. 28:13–15)

When Jacob awakes, he declares, "This is none other than the house of God" (v. 17), and he renames the place Bethel. It is where God will later rename *him* (Gen. 35:1–15).

Ai is famous for its destruction at the hands of Joshua who, on the second attempt, rendered it "a permanent heap of ruins" (Josh. 8:28 NIV). Thus, the names of both places turn out to be prophetic: *House of God* is where heaven touches earth, and *Ruin* is destroyed forever.

READ: Ephesians 1
REFLECT: Psalm 9:10
PRAY: Ask the Lord to help you worship Him wherever you are today, whether with believers or with unbelievers.

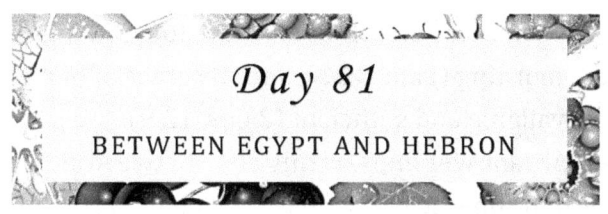

Day 81
BETWEEN EGYPT AND HEBRON

After the sojourn in Egypt, Abram returns to this area between Bethel and Ai and once again worships at the altar he had built earlier (Gen. 13:2). It must have been a relief to be back in a familiar place after what had transpired in Egypt: as we saw on Day 17, Pharaoh had unwittingly separated husband and wife by taking Sarai into his harem, and then unceremoniously expelled them from his land. Abram's second time at this altar between Bethel and Ai must have been marked with thanksgiving.

The primary significance of this altar is that Abram is in transition. He has just returned from the long trip to Egypt but has yet to find a permanent place to pitch his tent in Canaan. That place will be Hebron, but he does not know this yet. Abram must have felt somewhat unsettled, yet he remains faithful in worship. Thus, a key lesson of this altar is that it is necessary to be consistent in worship, even when we are in a transition of some kind—locational, vocational, relational, or other. We must diligently guard our time with the Lord and not let external circumstances dictate our inner life.

The devil will do everything in his power to steal our devotional time, which is why it requires a commitment on our part. We have to determine to press on without letting failures derail us. Regardless of how humdrum our devotional time was yesterday, we can start afresh every day, for God's mercies are new every morning (Lam. 3:23), and the grace of our Lord Jesus is always available and sufficient (2 Cor. 12:9).

When Abram worships at this altar between Bethel and Ai for the second time, he is also in transition in that he is between two situations of strife. He is barely recovering from what happened in Egypt when the herdsmen's strife looms on the horizon. No doubt this caused him some stress, but Abram finds his peace in God's presence. What Isaiah would declare centuries later is true of Abram: "You will keep him in perfect peace whose mind is stayed on you, because he trusts in you" (Is. 26:3 ESV).

We always hope that life will be smooth sailing after a rough spell, but unfortunately this is not always the case. At times we move from one trial to the next without a pause, and sometimes the trials overlap. Our only refuge is the presence of God, and if we are faithful to show up at the altar daily, we will receive the strength to face the challenges before us.

As we spend time with God, He will also give us the solutions we need. It is not difficult to imagine that as Abram prayed about the situation with the herdsmen, the Holy Spirit prompted him to address the matter with Lot and suggest a separation, thereby bringing an end to the strife.

> *READ: Ephesians 2*
> *REFLECT: Isaiah 26:3*
> *PRAY: Think of a situation of strife—in your own life or in the world—and pray for God's peace to reign.*

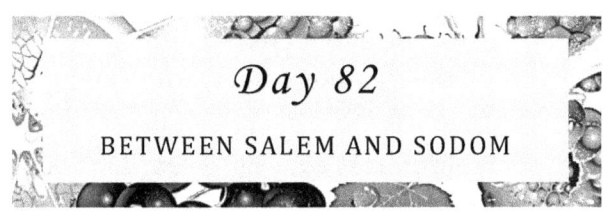

Day 82
BETWEEN SALEM AND SODOM

After Lot's fateful move to Sodom, the Lord again appears to Abram and promises the land to his descendants (Gen. 13:14–15). Earlier Lot had also lifted up his eyes and looked; but whereas Lot had looked and chosen for himself, Abram lifted up his eyes and saw the land that *God* had chosen for him.

Faith involves trusting God's choice, not just His timing. The best example of such a life is not Abraham but his greatest descendant, our Lord Jesus, who lived in total obedience to the Father's will from start to finish. Three times in Gethsemane, moments before His arrest, Jesus prayed, "Father, if it is possible, let this cup pass from Me; *nevertheless, not as I will, but as You will*" (Matt. 26:39,42,44).

When God appears to Abram after the separation from Lot, He confirms His word about descendants, and this time He elaborates on the earlier statement. Not only will there be descendants, but they will be *"as the dust of the earth"* (Gen. 13:16). In response, Abram moves near the oaks of Mamre in Hebron and once again builds an altar.

Hebron's geographical location is significant, for it lies midway between Salem and Sodom. As we know, Salem or Jerusalem is the city that will endure for all eternity, and Sodom has long since been destroyed and turned into the Dead Sea. The Hebron altar thus represents the place between life and death, between the final reward of the righteous and the final judgment of the wicked.

Another point of contrast between Salem and Sodom is apparent from the actions of their kings: whereas Melchizedek blesses Abram and God, Bera only has his own agenda in mind. Like Abram, we all know people who will openhandedly bless us and those who will manipulate, exploit, or harm us. How we worship God in an imperfect world reveals a great deal about our faith.

Apart from its physical location, the significance of the Hebron altar also lies in the personal crossroads Abram is at. It is the last altar we see him build while he is still childless, between God's promise of descendants and the birth of Isaac. Thus, the Hebron altar teaches us how to live in the interstitial place between God's promise and its fulfillment. Instead of trying to make the promise happen, we must faithfully build an altar to the Lord, *continually* offering "the sacrifice of praise, that is, the fruit of our lips" (Heb. 13:15).

While we are to actively seek God for His blessings, and while we can often hasten their arrival through faith, patience, and obedience, we must never let them usurp His place in our hearts. And as the Hebron altar reminds us, we must live in this manner *while we are waiting.*

READ: Ephesians 3
REFLECT: Hebrews 13:15
PRAY: Think of someone who seems to wish you ill and ask the Lord to bless them.

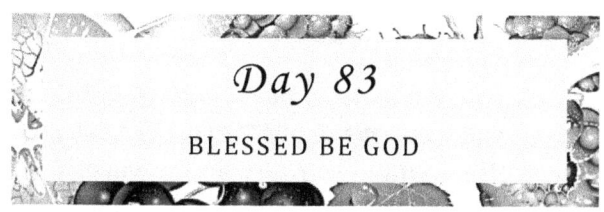

Day 83

BLESSED BE GOD

After blessing Abram, Melchizedek blesses God for a very specific reason. Like him, we too must be specific when we pray.

People who find prayer boring are usually making vague, formulaic prayers, mostly comprising stock phrases they picked up somewhere. If a normal human conversation fizzles out if it remains at the level of cliché, as theorists call the superficial level of communication, then conversation with the One we cannot see will definitely do likewise if it is no more than a formula.

Formulas are for infants. If we want to mature in our relationship with God, our prayers must move past ritualistic repetitions —and this includes liturgy. Whether it is quoted verbatim from Scripture, or whether it is drawn from inspired writings by godly people, liturgy can make us think we have "done our duty." Over time, it can also acquire an incantational aura, so that we think if we just say this prayer or make that declaration, what we need or want will be ours.

Making declarations according to God's Word is not wrong. In fact, it's something every believer *must* do, for it is a form of prayer. But our motive must be God's glory: as Jesus has said, "Whatever you ask in My name, that I will do, *that the Father may be glorified in the Son*" (John 14:13). Our declarations must also be made in the context of a relationship with God that is based on obedience. Jesus concludes the Sermon on the Mount with these sobering words:

> Not everyone who says to Me, "Lord, Lord," shall enter the kingdom of heaven, but he who does the will of My Father in heaven. Many will say to Me in that day, "Lord, Lord, have we not prophesied . . ., cast out demons . . ., and done many wonders in Your name?" And then I will declare to them, "I never knew you; depart from Me, you who practice lawlessness!" (Matt. 7:21–23)

For Jesus, prophesying, casting out demons, and doing many wonders—*even in His name*—is not as important as doing the will of His Father. And not doing the will of His Father is equivalent to practicing lawlessness.

Certain kinds of prayers may indeed get us what we want, but is that enough? Or is the kingdom of heaven the pearl of great price, the treasure we are to desire above all other treasures? It is. And Jesus has categorically stated that *only doing the will of His Father* will get us into the kingdom of heaven.

Liturgy and doing the will of the Father are not mutually exclusive. They can definitely coexist. Nor are liturgy and the *rhema* word mutually exclusive. In fact, at times liturgy *is* the *rhema*, the specific word God gives for a particular situation. The problem is not liturgy. The problem is *reducing liturgy to a formula*, and letting it replace a live conversation with God, where we praise Him for something current, and hear what He is saying *right now*, as Melchizedek did.

> *READ: Ephesians 4*
> *REFLECT: Matthew 7:21*
> *PRAY: Praise God for something current, and speak to Him from your heart, as though you'd talk to a friend.*

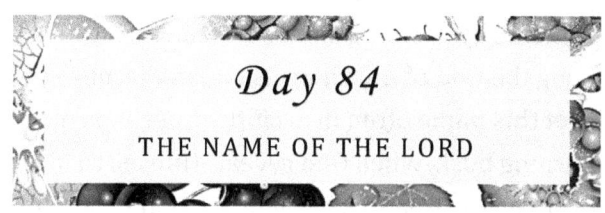

Day 84

THE NAME OF THE LORD

Melchizedek's second statement reminds us of the importance of blessing God. We can never out-bless God, because He blesses us immeasurably more than we could ever bless Him. Nevertheless, we must still bless God with our whole being: as Psalm 103 urges, "Bless the LORD, O my soul; And all that is within me, bless His holy name!" (vv. 1–2).

Believers fall into two categories: those who bless God "at all times" and "continually" (Ps. 34:1), and those who only bless Him when things are going well—or, conversely, when things are going badly and they need God's help. Once He delivers them, they vanish like the nine ungrateful lepers in Luke 17.

The tenth leper, seeing that he has been healed, glorifies God loudly, falls at Jesus' feet, and thanks Him. In response Jesus says, "Your faith has made you well" (v. 19). The other nine were also healed by believing in Jesus' word, but only *this* man's faith received His commendation, because only *he* expressed his faith by blessing God.

Melchizedek is not the first person in Scripture to bless God. That distinction belongs to Noah. After he learns how his son Ham had dishonored him, Noah pronounces a curse on Ham's son Canaan and then proclaims, "Blessed be the LORD, the God of Shem" (Gen. 9:26). Since Shem will become the ancestor of Abraham,

Isaac, and Jacob, by blessing the God of Shem, Noah is prophetically blessing the God of Abraham, Isaac, and Jacob.

We meet this name often in Scripture, perhaps most famously at the burning bush, when God reveals Himself to Moses as "the God of Abraham, the God of Isaac and the God of Jacob" (Ex. 3:6). While discussing the faith of the three patriarchs, the writer of Hebrews will say that God is "not ashamed to be called their God" (Heb. 11:16).

Jesus' own Hebrew name, Yeshua, is a form of Yehoshua, which means *salvation* and is derived from God's covenant name, Yahweh, plus the verb *yasha*, which means to help, deliver, save, or rescue.

After Pentecost, the apostles preach and perform miracles in the name of Jesus, and the church multiplies rapidly as a result. The first healing miracle recorded in the book of Acts takes place at the Temple in Jerusalem, when Peter tells the lame beggar, "Silver and gold I do not have, but what I have I give you. In the name of Jesus Christ of Nazareth, walk" (Acts 3:6). Next day, when the Sanhedrin ask Peter and John by what name they had healed the lame man, Peter replies,

> It is by the name of Jesus Christ of Nazareth.... Salvation is found in no one else, for there is no other name under heaven given to mankind by which we must be saved. (Acts 4: 10,12 NIV)

READ: Ephesians 5
REFLECT: Psalm 103:1–2
PRAY: Ask God to help you bless Him continually today, and pray for some need in the name of Jesus.

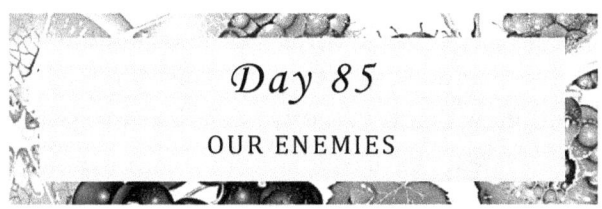

Day 85

OUR ENEMIES

In Genesis 14:20 Melchizedek blesses God for delivering Abram's enemies into his hand. It is the first time the word enemies appears in Scripture, and it is the first time *people* are said to be delivered into people's hands. Earlier, God had delivered the living creatures into Noah's hand (Gen. 9:2). Since God has handed Abram's enemies to him, according to the blessing of Melchizedek Abram is the first victor in the Bible. In this he typifies Christ, the greatest victor of all time.

While Abram's enemies were Chedorlaomer and his allies, from Jesus' parable about the sower and the seed (Mark 4:3–20), we learn that our enemies are *the world, the flesh, and the devil*.

When He explains the parable to the disciples, Jesus tells them that the seed is the word of God. Since we live by "every word that proceeds from the mouth of the Lord" (Deut. 8:3), our three enemies seek to snatch it from us so we will not lead abundant, fruitful lives.

In Jesus' parable, the birds of the air that devour the seed fallen by the wayside represent *the devil*, whose sole mission is to keep the word of God from even entering a person's heart. God's word is the truth, and knowing the truth sets us free (John 8:32), whereas the devil wants to keep us bound with his lies. In Jesus' words, he is "a liar and the father of it" (v. 44).

The seed that falls on stony ground is unable to grow roots because of the shallowness of the soil. This symbolizes *the flesh*, the force within us that constantly seeks its own gratification. It resents the slightest degree of discomfort and will cause a weak Christian to fall away in times of persecution.

The last of the bad soils in Jesus' parable, the thorns that choke the seed that has fallen among them, represents "the cares of this world, the deceitfulness of riches, and the desires for other things" (Mark 4:19). This is a picture of *the world*, with its insistent demands and allurements, all designed to seduce us away from God. The world also stands for its systems, beliefs, and ideologies, all of which are contrary to how the kingdom of God operates.

In Psalm 116, written to thank God for deliverance, the psalmist declares, "You have delivered my soul from death, my eyes from tears, and my feet from stumbling" (v. 8). These woes—death, tears, and stumbling—are the deeds of our enemies. Death is a work of the devil, tears come from what we experience in the world, and we stumble because our flesh is weak—but Jesus has delivered us from them all!

Just as the Lord enabled Abram to triumph over his enemies, He gives us victory over *our* enemies: as Paul declared, "Thanks be to God who *always* leads us in triumph in Christ" (2 Cor. 2:14). If we are trusting in Jesus's work on the cross for our victory, this is true of us.

READ: Ephesians 6
REFLECT: Romans 8:37
PRAY: Think of an area where you need to be a conqueror and ask God to help you take one step of victory today.

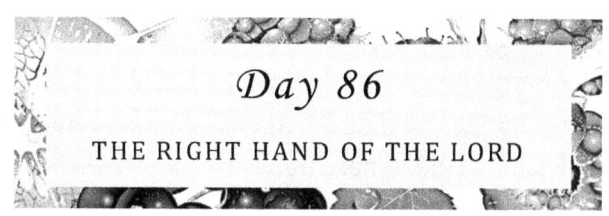

Day 86
THE RIGHT HAND OF THE LORD

Abram's rescue of Lot, the event that immediately precedes the blessing of Melchizedek, foreshadows the cross. This makes Melchizedek's second statement prophetic: when he blessed God Most High for delivering Abram's enemies into his hand, Melchizedek was also foretelling what God would do for Abram's greatest descendant. Centuries later David would prophesy the same thing in Psalm 110:1,

> The LORD said to my Lord,
> "Sit at My right hand,
> Till I make Your enemies Your footstool."

The right hand of God represents three things. First, it is *the place where Jesus is seated in heaven*, having successfully completed His atoning work. A king's right hand is the position of highest honor, and Jesus alone deserves this place in the eternal throne room. Shortly before His crucifixion He had announced, "Hereafter the Son of Man will sit at the right hand of the power of God" (Luke 22:69). The earliest Gospel closes by saying that after His ascension Jesus "was received up into heaven, and sat down at the right hand of God" (Mark 16:19); and the epistles refer to Jesus' station often (e.g., Rom. 8:34; Eph. 1:20; Col. 3:1; Heb. 1:13; 10:12; 12:2; 1 Pet. 3:22).

The Lord's right hand also symbolizes *Jesus' rulership*, for it is in His right hand that He holds the scepter or rod of authority. On Day 49 we had noted that David uses the same Hebrew word, *mattah*, in Psalm 110:2, where he prophesies that the rod of the Messiah's power will be sent out from Zion. As we saw, *mattah* is used variously as a branch for chastening, a scepter for ruling, and a staff for walking; but the sense in Psalm 110:2 is that of *rulership*. Held in the Messiah's right hand, the rod is an emblem of His royal power, and that power will go forth from Jerusalem. Having seen this by the Spirit, David joyously exhorts his greatest descendant, "Rule in the midst of Your enemies!"

Finally, the right hand of God is *a messianic term*. Jesus Himself is the right hand of God! The title appears every so often in Old Testament songs and prophecies. For example, after the crossing of the Red Sea, Moses and the Israelites sang, "Your right hand, LORD, was majestic in power. Your right hand, LORD, shattered the enemy" (Ex. 15:6 NIV). And in Isaiah 41:10 the Lord assures His people,

> Fear not, for I am with you; Be not dismayed, for I am your God. I will strengthen you, Yes, I will help you, I will uphold you with My righteous right hand.

Jesus is the righteous right hand who strengthens, helps, and upholds the people of God.

READ: James 1
REFLECT: Isaiah 41:10
PRAY: Think of a time when the Lord's right hand saved or upheld you, and thank Him for it.

Part Five

THE RESPONSE

And [Abram] gave [Melchizedek] a tithe of all.
Now the king of Sodom said to Abram, "Give me the persons, and take the goods for yourself."
But Abram said to the king of Sodom, "I have raised my hand to the LORD, God Most High, the Possessor of heaven and earth, that I will take nothing, from a thread to a sandal strap, and that I will not take anything that is yours, lest you should say, 'I have made Abram rich'— except only what the young men have eaten, and the portion of the men who went with me: Aner, Eshcol, and Mamre; let them take their portion."
After these things the word of the LORD came to Abram in a vision, saying, "Do not be afraid, Abram. I am your shield, your exceedingly great reward."

—GENESIS 14:19–15:1

Whom have I in heaven but You? And there is none upon earth that I desire besides You. My heart and my flesh fail; But God is the strength of my heart and my portion forever.

—PSALM 73:25–26

Walk worthy of the calling with which you were called.

—EPHESIANS 4:1

Fruitful Days
87–97

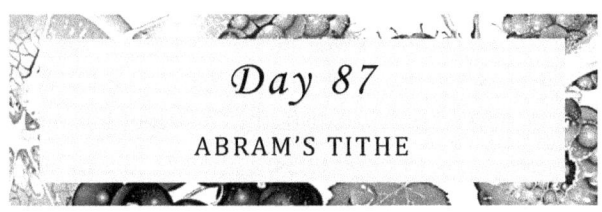

Day 87
ABRAM'S TITHE

Every blessing demands a response, and the first thing Abram does after being blessed is give Melchizedek a tithe. Hebrews 7:4 specifies that this was a tenth of the spoils. Abram could have kept it all for himself, but he holds things lightly because he loves God, not goods. He also recognizes that he owes Melchizedek a tithe. Not only must he thank him for the blessing, but he must also pay him a tribute, for as a king and priest, Melchizedek is his superior.

In Genesis 14:20 we have the first mention of tithing in Scripture. The next is when Jacob promises to give God a tenth of all that God will give him (Gen. 28:22). As a law, the tithe is introduced in Leviticus 27:30, where Moses says, "All the tithe of the land, whether of the seed of the land or of the fruit of the tree, is the LORD's. It is holy to the LORD." In ancient Israel the tithe was a means of providing for the priests and of helping those who found themselves in poverty.

The best-known passage on the tithe appears in the penultimate chapter of the Old Testament:

> Will a man rob God? Yet you have robbed Me! But you say, "In what way have we robbed You?" In tithes and offerings. You are cursed with a curse, For you have robbed Me. (Mal. 3:8–9)

God described the withholding of the tithe as robbery because the tithe belonged to Him, and the eighth commandment prohibits theft. To violate any commandment is to invoke a curse on oneself. On the contrary, when a person gives to the priests, a blessing will rest on their house (Ezek. 44:30). This is not to suggest that if we tithe we will all become rich and God will never test us in the area of finances. In fact, the one area in which He usually *does* test our faith is our finances.

In the New Testament we find that Jesus never did away with the tithe, even though He rebuked the Pharisees for tithing with exactitude while neglecting the more crucial aspects of the law: justice, mercy, and faith (Matt. 23:23). Some people believe that the tithe is not mandatory for new covenant believers, but anyone who understands how much God has given and forgiven them will rather err on the side of generosity. Conversely, as Jesus says, "Whoever has been forgiven little loves little" (Luke 7:47 NIV).

A fundamental principle of sowing and reaping is that we reap what we sow. Therefore, if we want to reap bountifully from God, we should be unstinting when we give to Him.

The last mention of the tithe in Scripture, like the first, is connected with Melchizedek. It appears in Hebrews 7, where Abram's tithe is used to prove Jesus' superiority as our High Priest, as we saw on Day 52. The bottom line is that gratitude for our Lord's atoning work on our behalf will govern all our behavior, *including our giving*.

> *READ: James 2*
> *REFLECT: Luke 6:38*
> *PRAY: Ask God to help you be more generous, financially and otherwise, and be more generous today.*

Day 88

OBJECTIONS TO TITHING

Christians who object to tithing do so for at least four reasons. Two of these are overt, and most people readily admit to them. The other two are internal, and people will own up to them with reluctance—if at all.

The internal objections lie at the heart level, the level God is more interested in. This is why Solomon urged us to guard our heart *above all else*, "for out of it spring the issues of life" (Prov. 4:23). Once we deal with the issues of the heart, it will be easier to deal with the overt objections.

The first internal reason why people object to tithing is unbelief. Most Christians, especially those who have followed Jesus for some length of time, find it difficult to admit that they struggle with unbelief; but beneath the withholding of the tithe is an inability to take God at His word. Since God has said He will bless obedience, we must be willing to believe Him and live accordingly.

The object of our faith must be God. When a person lacks faith in God, they are usually placing too much faith in *themselves*. Deep down they believe their own wisdom, education, talent, strength, or hard work has brought (or will bring) them blessing. While God certainly blesses us when we use the gifts He has given us, we must never forget that He is one who gave them to us in the first place. Our very *breath* is His gift.

Apart from ourselves, we can also make other people the object of our faith. This renders them an idol, and we must guard our heart against idolatry especially with respect to our needs. As we noted on Day 79, an idol is something to which a person turns to meet a need. If we have a tendency to first turn to others and last to God, we must diligently cultivate a habit of *first* turning to God. And this applies to all our needs, material and tangible or otherwise.

While on the topic of unbelief, we must remember that the source of unbelief is the devil, whom Jesus Himself calls "the father of lies" (John 8:44). When the devil talks against us to God he sticks to the facts, because he accuses us on the basis of our sins. But when he talks against God to us, he *never* sticks to the facts. He *always* lies to us about God. If we believe him, as our first parents did, we will hurtle headlong into unbelief, for unbelief is nothing but believing the lie about God and not believing the truth about Him.

We cannot *not* believe. We must believe *something*—and our only options are the lie or the truth. We believe either what the devil tells us about God, or what God tells us about Himself. If Abraham's believing what the Lord had said was credited to him as righteousness, then a person's *not* believing the word of the Lord is credited to them as *un*righteousness. Which is a big word for a small word: sin.

READ: *James 3*
REFLECT: *Philippians 4:19*
PRAY: *Ask God to show you one area where you have been trusting in yourself or others, and ask His forgiveness.*

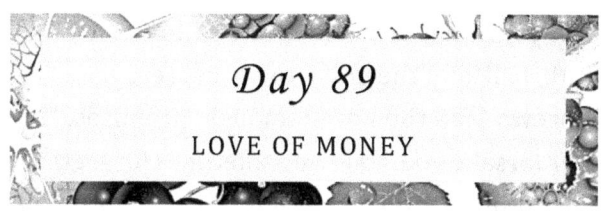

Day 89
LOVE OF MONEY

Those who object to tithing usually love money too much to part with it. And it may well be that God has instituted the tithe partly to rid His people of the love of money, to keep us free from loving and depending on money instead of Him.

Solomon, who apart from his great wisdom was also one of the wealthiest men in history, had this to say about loving money: "He who loves silver will not be satisfied with silver" (Eccl. 5:10). He could have left it at "will not be satisfied," but he added "with silver" to tell us that those who love money will, paradoxically, not be satisfied *with money*. And this is true whether the lover of money is a spendthrift or a miser.

The spendthrift never has enough to spend, and the miser never has enough to save. Thus, neither can be satisfied with the money they have. This is why Jesus has told us to store our treasures in heaven, because our heart will be wherever our treasure is (Matt. 6:20–21).

We can also infer from Ecclesiastes 5:10 that the one who does *not* love money *will* be satisfied with it. When such a person gets money, they spend it and save it as needed and there the matter rests. It goes from their wallet to wherever it is needed, bypassing their heart. Such a person understands that money was not meant to satisfy the heart. The only thing that can satisfy our deepest yearnings is the love of God in Christ, the love that defied death, hell, and the grave to set us free.

In Hebrews 13:5 the Lord famously promises, "I will never leave you or forsake you," but we sometimes forget that the verse opens with an injunction concerning the love of money: "Keep your life free from the love of money, and be content with what you have" (ESV). If we truly believe that our Father will never forsake us, we will demonstrate it by not clinging to money as our source of worth, security, and provision.

"The love of money is a root of all kinds of evil," says Paul in 1 Timothy 6:10. Certain kinds of evil do not stem from this root, and there are other roots of evil apart from the love of money. Even so, that this root produces *any* evil, let alone *all kinds of evil*, makes it serious enough. Nor must we forget that Jesus has said, "No one can serve two masters.... You cannot serve God and money" (Matt. 6:24 ESV).

God knows that the love of money will keep us from enjoying life to the fullest, and this pure, unadulterated joy is God's desire for us here on earth, even before we experience the fullness of joy in heaven. Jesus wants His disciples' joy to be *full* and *complete* (John 15:11; 16:24), and only someone with this kind of joy can be the cheerful giver that God loves (2 Cor. 9:7). God loves cheerful givers because He loves cheerful *giving*, for that reflects His own style of giving.

READ: James 4
REFLECT: Matthew 6:24
PRAY: If the love of money has produced any evil in your life, ask the Lord to forgive you and set you free.

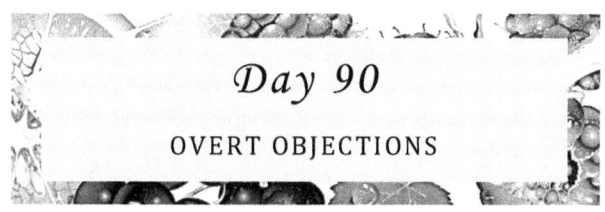

Day 90
OVERT OBJECTIONS

The first overt objection to tithing is that it's legalism, and we are "not under the law, but under grace." But as we noted on Day 28, the previous clause of Romans 6:14 is "Sin shall not have dominion over you." That's what this verse is about.

Those who object to tithing on grounds of legalism prove that they do not in fact understand what *grace* is. Grace is not the right to do what one pleases; it is *the power to do what pleases God*. Grace is not freedom from all obligations; it is *the freedom to fulfill the right obligations*.

Tithing is not legalism any more than being faithful to one's spouse or not murdering someone is not legalism. What is legalism is to *legislate* tithing, and to impose it on others. Everyone must make the choice for themselves. Moses himself implied this in one of the last things he said:

> I have set before you life and death, blessing and curses. *Now choose* life, so that you and your children may live and that you may love the LORD your God, listen to his voice, and hold fast to him. For the LORD is your life. (Deut. 30:19–20 NIV)

Someone who does not tithe on grounds of legalism is correct to say, "It's legalism *to enforce the tithe on me*," but they are wrong to say, "It's legalism *for me to tithe*." They may still choose not to tithe, but that is not full, wholehearted obedience, and those who hold back from fully obeying God are only shortchanging themselves. Ultimately, whoever withholds the tithe is robbing themselves of the blessing God places on the remaining nine-tenths.

The second overt objection to tithing is that it does not make sense. This objection makes perfect sense when said from a purely human perspective, but God's perspective is completely different from ours. As He says in Isaiah 55:9, "As the heavens are higher than the earth, so are My ways higher than your ways, and My thoughts than your thoughts."

Since our Lord's kingdom is "not of this world" (John 18:36), life in His kingdom does not operate in terms of how the systems of this world operate. That's why it takes faith to be a citizen of the kingdom of God. Not only do we *enter* it by faith, but we also *live* in it by faith.

I am not making a case for the tithe so much as I am for faith and obedience. God does not need our money but we need His blessings, and He can bless us most lavishly when we are living in a manner that pleases Him. When we live in such a manner, we can confidently ask Him for blessings: as 1 John 3:22 says, "Whatever we ask we receive from Him, because we keep His commandments and do those things that are pleasing in His sight."

> READ: James 5
> REFLECT: Isaiah 55:9
> PRAY: Ask the Lord to show you one thing you need to see from His perspective today.

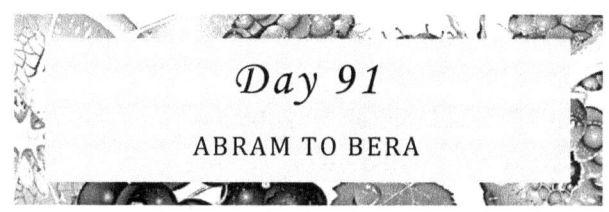

Day 91

ABRAM TO BERA

After Abram receives the blessing of Melchizedek, Bera king of Sodom makes him an offer: Keep the spoils of war, return the people. Abram puts his rejection of this offer in the form of an oath, saying, "I have raised my hand to the LORD" (Gen. 14:22). He is calling God to witness his words. He does not need to put his statement in writing, because he knows that God sees and hears everything. By contrast, many Christians today behave in the contractual manner of the world. They make promises verbally, but as long as nothing is written down, they feel they have the option to back out.

Jesus' statement in the Sermon on the Mount, "Let your 'Yes' be 'Yes,' and your 'No,' 'No'" (Matt. 5:37), is often used to teach that we must never make oaths. But what our Lord was prohibiting was swearing by heaven, earth, Jerusalem, or one's own head. *Those* are the oaths we are to avoid—the kind that need to be bolstered by something beyond our personal integrity. Jesus is also saying that our yes *should be yes*, and our no *should be no*. We should mean what we say and say what we mean.

As the people of God we must only make promises we have the intention of keeping, not because we want people to like us or feel beholden to us. And when we say we will do something, we must do it. Since God is omniscient and omnipresent, anything we say or do is done with His knowledge. Therefore, whatever we say, we are saying before God.

In Psalm 15 David makes two observations about those who keep their word: they will dwell in the presence of the Lord; and they will never be moved (vv. 1,5). David was a man who both dwelt in God's presence and who was not moved, even in the most daunting of circumstances. If we want these two benefits, we too must take our word seriously.

Being true to our word is a hallmark of integrity. The corruption rampant in virtually every sphere of society indicates that the world is facing an acute shortage of integrity. On the surface, the lack of integrity is a discrepancy between word and deed, but at a deeper level it is a disconnect between what one pretends to be and what one really is. It is this hypocrisy that Jesus condemned when He referred to the scribes and Pharisees as "whitewashed tombs which indeed appear beautiful outwardly, but inside are full of dead men's bones and all uncleanness" (Matt. 23:27).

Such an external righteousness will not count for eternity. As Jesus had said in Matthew 5:20, one will never enter the kingdom of heaven unless one's righteousness exceeds that of the scribes and Pharisees.

READ: 1 Peter 1
REFLECT: Matthew 5:37
PRAY: If you have failed to keep your word to someone, ask them to forgive you.

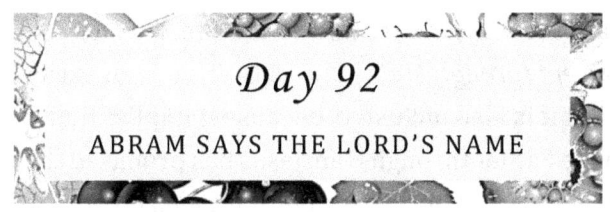

Day 92
ABRAM SAYS THE LORD'S NAME

When Abram responds to Bera, he uses Melchizedek's term for God: "God Most High, the Possessor of heaven and earth." Melchizedek has given him a new revelation of God, and Abram applies it right away.

It is imperative to apply revelation to life without letting time go by. When we apply what we know of God it becomes more deeply entrenched in us, and that paves the way for us to receive more. In Matthew 24 Jesus tells the parable of the faithful servant, the moral of which is that those who are faithful with little will be entrusted with more. That our Lord told this parable while discussing the signs of the end times suggests that faithfulness in small things will be one of the big virtues in the last days.

Before Abram uses the term he has learnt from Melchizedek, he uses the name he already knows: the Lord (Yahweh). In all likelihood, as the king of a city like Sodom, Bera has no real knowledge of Yahweh, though he may have heard of Him. Nevertheless, Abram is unafraid to utter the Lord's name in Bera's presence. For us this means being unafraid to say the name of Jesus.

It's far easier to say "God" in the presence of those who do not have a personal knowledge of Jesus, but to say "Jesus" is another matter, for it identifies us as Christians—and true Christians believe that Jesus is the *only* way to the Father. As Jesus Himself said, "I am the way, the truth, and the life. No one comes to the Father *except through Me*" (John 14:6). That is an exclusive statement—but it is also *in*clusive, because it implies that *anyone* can come to the Father through Him. Jesus has promised that *whoever* believes in Him will not perish but have everlasting life (John 3:16).

The hostility towards our Lord's name is escalating, and anyone who claims to be a follower of Jesus must be willing to suffer for His name. The early disciples left a scene of persecution "rejoicing that they were counted worthy to suffer shame for His name" (Acts 5:41), and the time is not far off when many of us will have to do likewise.

When we identify ourselves as Christians, people will think of us as anything from odd to intolerant, and they may even mock or persecute us outright. But we will never be effective in our witness unless we take the name of Jesus, because without Him there is no gospel: as Peter boldly tells the Jewish leaders, "There is no other name under heaven given among men by which we must be saved" (Acts 4:12).

Moreover, Jesus has warned that if we are ashamed of Him before people, He will be ashamed of us before the Father (Luke 9:26). It is far better to risk the rejection of those who can only harm the body than that of "Him who can destroy both soul and body in hell" (Matt. 10:28).

READ: 1 Peter 2
REFLECT: Luke 9:26
PRAY: Ask the Lord to give you the boldness to tell someone about Jesus—by name—today.

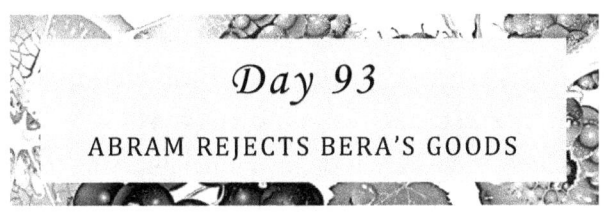

Day 93
ABRAM REJECTS BERA'S GOODS

Abram rejects Bera's offer because he does not want Bera to claim, "I have made Abram rich" (Gen. 14:23). Abram wants God to make him rich, because the Possessor of heaven and earth is the true source of wealth. Nevertheless, Abram acts shrewdly on behalf of his allies. Since it would be unfair to deny the Amorite brothers their share of the spoils, he tells Bera, "Let them take their portion."

Genesis 14:24 gives us the first instance of the word portion. In this context, the Hebrew term refers to the booty, but the root from which it is derived, *cheleq*, also means inheritance. The word is used variously in the Old Testament. For instance, the Lord Himself is known as "the Portion of Jacob" (Jer. 10:16), and the psalmist declares, "God is the strength of my heart and my portion forever" (Ps. 73:26). The truth that God is our portion is a key concept to understand when we are seeking to learn what God has for us.

When we know the Lord as the Possessor of heaven and earth, and when we understand how deeply He has loved us in sacrificing His only Son for us, it will free us from looking to people to provide for us. It will also keep us from competing with others for blessing. The competitive spirit, which Western individualism has perfected, is unfortunately also prevalent in the church, whereas the body of Christ is to "have the same mindset as Christ" (Phil. 2:5 NIV). We are to consider others above ourselves and to look to their interests, not just our own (v. 4).

If we believe that there is only so much blessing to go around, and that if someone else is blessed then our own portion will be reduced, we will compete and scramble for the biggest portion. This stems from what some call "the orphan spirit," the mentality of those who believe they have no one to provide for them—even though Jesus has clearly said, "Your Father knows the things you have need of before you ask Him" (Matt. 6:8). Paul will later affirm this truth: "He who did not spare His own Son, but delivered Him over for us all, *how will He not also with Him freely give us all things?*" (Rom. 8:32 NASB).

We can only live in total security with respect to our inheritance when we are convinced that God is our Father and that He has more than enough blessing to go around. It is also critical to remember that the greatest obstacle to getting our portion is our own lack of faith and obedience.

Knowing that our heavenly Father has the best for us will prevent us from coveting what others have, and it will also keep us from accepting everything that comes our way, for not everything that *looks* good *is* good. As Abram had wisely discerned, Sodom's goods were not good.

READ: 1 Peter 3
REFLECT: Psalm 73:26
PRAY: Ask God to forgive you if you have competed with others for blessing and confess Him as your portion today.

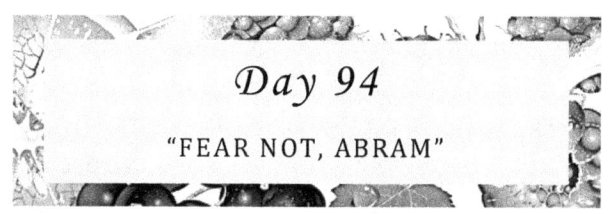

Day 94

"FEAR NOT, ABRAM"

Genesis 14 closes with Abram speaking to Bera king of Sodom, rejecting his offer, and Genesis 15 opens with the Lord visiting Abram in a vision and saying, "Fear not, Abram, I am your shield; your reward shall be very great" (Gen. 15:1 ESV).

Here we have the first of the many "Fear nots" of the Bible. Despite the faith and courage Abram had already displayed, for some reason he needed reassurance at this point. And so God visits him with a word, just as He also meets us in our fears by speaking to us. The One who said "Fear not, for I am with you" (Is. 43:5) is Immanuel, God *with* us, and if we are willing to listen He is willing to speak.

Genesis 15:1 is also the first instance where we find the Lord addressing Abram by name. "Fear not, *Abram*," He says, which makes the statement extremely personal. It is said to a *particular* man with a *particular* fear. Abram's fear, as we learn from his response in verse 2, is that he will die childless.

Those who don't understand God's heart or the way He works in our lives may think it was cruel or unfair of Him to promise Abraham descendants and then make him wait twenty-five years. Apart from having an incorrect view of God, such people don't believe the promise in Isaiah 40:31, that "those who wait on the Lord shall renew their strength."

Waiting in human terms is enervating, but waiting on the Lord is energizing—partly because the strength to wait comes from Him, and partly because we don't have to wonder if He will come through or not. When we wait on the Lord, we are not waiting for a human being who may let us down. God *cannot* fail, for faithfulness is the foundation of His throne (Ps. 89:14). He can never be anything other than faithful: as Paul asserts, "If we are faithless, *He remains faithful, for He cannot deny Himself*" (2 Tim. 2:13 NASB). Unlike a human being who may forget or lose track of time or be delayed by forces beyond their control, the Lord has no such limitations. Moreover, though people may change their mind about what they have promised, God never does.

When the Moabite king Balak asked Balaam the seer to curse Israel, Balaam would only utter what the Lord put in his mouth. One of those words was this: "God is not human, that he should lie. . . . Does he speak and then not act? Does he promise and not fulfill?" (Num. 23:19–20 NIV).

The fact that God does not change His mind about what He has promised is as much a part of His character as any other attribute revealed in Scripture. Therefore, if we fail to receive His promises, it is through our own fault. The most common mistakes we make are trying to obtain the promises our way instead of God's, and giving up.

READ: 1 Peter 4
REFLECT: Isaiah 43:5
PRAY: Tell the Lord you will obtain His promises His way, not yours, and ask Him for the grace not to give up.

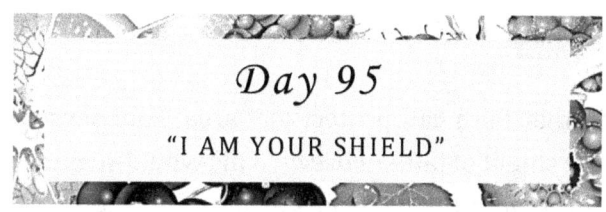

Day 95
"I AM YOUR SHIELD"

Genesis 15:1 is the first time we hear the Lord using the words "I am" to someone. Melchizedek had earlier affirmed Abram's relationship with God by blessing him in the name of God Most High. Now God Himself affirms that relationship by telling Abram who He is to him: "I am your shield."

It is significant that the Lord calls Himself Abram's shield shortly after he has emerged from battle. The shield is among the most important pieces of a soldier's armor, and Abram is now in a better position to appreciate the Lord as his shield. The Hebrew word for shield, *magen*, derives from the verb *ganan*, meaning to cover, surround, and defend. The psalmists frequently refer to the Lord as the shield, meaning that He is to or gives to His people glory, favor, salvation, strength, help, authority, blessing, truth, protection, and deliverance.

The Greek word for shield, *thureos*, is used only once in the New Testament, in the spiritual warfare passage, where Paul lists the various items of the armor of God. When he gets to the shield he says, "Above all, [take up] the shield of faith with which you will be able to quench all the fiery darts of the enemy" (Eph. 6:16). The door-shaped shield of ancient Rome was large enough to provide full-body protection. Paul describes faith as the shield because the *thureos* guarded any exposed area—and that is exactly what faith does. It protects *any* area of our life that is under attack.

Given that faith can protect any area, Paul says we should take up the shield of faith *above all*. This would suggest that faith is *the most item* in the believer's armor. And the second "all" in Ephesians 6:16 tells us that faith enables us to resist *all* the fiery darts of the enemy. Not *some*, not *most*, but *all* of what the devil throws our way can be blocked by the shield of faith!

The imagery of fiery darts is drawn from ancient warfare. A dart was a light spear or arrow with a pointed shaft at one end; the other end had feathers, which were set alight as the dart was aimed. That is why Paul describes the devil's darts as *fiery* and says they must be *quenched*. When held in place, the shield bears the brunt of the dart's pointed shaft and it keeps the flames from scorching the target.

While under attack, we must never forget that the fiery darts are coming from hell, and hell is a place where "the fire is not quenched," as Isaiah 66:24 says. Jesus quoted this verse three times in Mark 9, when warning about the reality of hell as the punishment for sin. The only time hell's fiery darts can be quenched is when we lift up the shield of faith here on earth. This is why we are urged to "hold fast the confession of our hope without wavering"—and we must do so all the more as we "see the Day approaching" (Heb. 10:23,25).

READ: 1 Peter 5
REFLECT: Ephesians 6:16
PRAY: Ask the Lord to show you one area where you need to lift up the shield of faith today, and lift it up.

Day 96
"YOUR REWARD"

Genesis 15:1 contains the first instance of the word reward, which is closely linked with the concept of blessing. While the general blessings of God are the result of common grace, and while we all receive the blessings that accompany salvation when we are saved, God's special blessings are *rewards*. We obtain them by living in a manner that pleases Him—and it is not surprising that *sakar*, the Hebrew word for reward in Genesis 15:1, means *wages*.

In Psalm 19 David extols God's laws as perfect, sure, right, pure, clean, true, righteous, more desirable than gold, and "sweeter also than honey and the honeycomb" (vv. 7–10). By them His servants are warned, and *"in keeping them there is great reward"* (v. 11). In other words, obedience to God's commandments causes us to inherit God's best blessings.

Jesus mentions seven rewards in Matthew—five in the Sermon on the Mount, and two in the instructions He gives His disciples before sending them out to preach. These rewards are given for enduring persecution, loving our enemies, doing charitable deeds in secret, praying in secret, fasting in secret, receiving a prophet and a righteous person, and giving to the disciples. Some rewards we will receive in this lifetime, but most of them will be ours only in eternity.

Our Lord has promised that when He returns, He will reward each person according to their works (Matt. 16:27). The wicked will be cast into hell, but the final reward for the redeemed is more than being taken up to heaven. It means that Jesus will judge our works and reward us accordingly, as 1 Corinthians 3:8 affirms. We will get a reward *only if our work endures*. Otherwise, although we ourselves will be saved, our works will be burned (vv. 14–15). This is why later in the same epistle Paul urges, "Run in such a way that you may obtain [the prize]" (1 Cor. 9:24).

Not every manner of running is prizeworthy, just as qualifying for the Olympics does not guarantee a medal. Not every runner who enters the races wins the gold, silver, or bronze. In fact, most competitors do *not* get a medal. This implies that there are only two styles of running: the style that wins the prize, and the one that does not. Paul took his race very seriously, and we too must "press toward the goal for the prize of the upward call of God in Christ Jesus" (Phil. 3:14).

If we believe everything else Jesus has said, we must also believe what He said in Matthew 16:27, that He will reward each person according to their works. And He has said this not only in the first book of the New Testament but also in the last. In the Bible's final chapter Jesus promises, "Behold, I am coming quickly, and My reward is with Me, to give to every one according to his work" (Rev. 22:12).

READ: *1 John 1*
REFLECT: *1 Corinthians 9:24*
PRAY: *Ask the Lord to show you where you are not running so as to obtain the prize, and change your style today.*

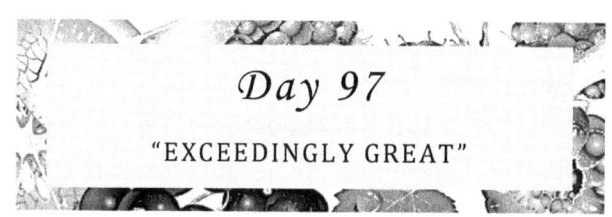

Day 97
"EXCEEDINGLY GREAT"

When God tells Abram about his reward, He does not say it is merely a reward or even a great reward. He says it will be *exceedingly great*. The Hebrew adjective, *meod*, means much-ness, force, and abundance. Webster defines our own word exceeding as "exceptional in amount, quality, or degree," and this is exactly what Abram's reward turns out to be.

When God tells Abram about his reward, Abram is moments away from displaying the faith that will be credited to him as righteousness. He had left Haran by faith, and he has lived by faith up to this point; but the faith he is about to display is the one that will *save* him, for that is what it means to have faith "credited as righteousness." When Paul writes to counter a heretical doctrine of salvation that has infiltrated the Galatian congregation, he quotes Genesis 15:6 and adds,

> *Only those who have faith are children of Abraham.* Scripture foresaw that God would justify the Gentiles by faith, and announced the gospel in advance to Abraham: "All nations will be blessed through you." So those who rely on faith are blessed along with Abraham, the man of faith. (Gal. 3:7–9 NIV)

The Greek word for exceedingly appears famously at the end of Paul's intercessory prayer in Ephesians 3. The apostle made this glorious prayer on his knees before the Father, "from whom the whole family in heaven and earth is named" (v. 15). Kneeling, as we noted on Day 2, is the best posture for obtaining a blessing —from our earthly parents and especially from our heavenly Father. We bow before God in worship because He is our King, but we can kneel before Him for blessing because He is our Father.

In Ephesians 3:16–19 Paul prays that God's Spirit will strengthen the believers so they will grasp the full measure of Christ's love and thus become filled "with all the fullness of God" (v. 19). The phrase "that you may be filled" appears again in Colossians 1:9, where the apostle speaks of praying that the believers will be filled with the knowledge of God's will. In Ephesians 3 the word exceedingly appears in the doxology that concludes Paul's prayer:

> Now to Him who is able to do *exceedingly abundantly above all that we ask or think*, according to the power that works in us, to Him be glory in the church by Christ Jesus to all generations, forever and ever. Amen. (vv. 20–21)

The text that follows "exceedingly" perfectly describes God's special blessings: they are immeasurably more than what we can ask or even imagine! When we find ourselves the recipients of such blessings, the result should always be praise and glory to the name of our Lord Jesus Christ.

READ: 1 John 2
REFLECT: Ephesians 3:20–21
PRAY: Thank God that He can do more than you can ask or imagine, and believe Him for a specific need today.

Epilogue

THE PROMISED SON

For unto us a Child is born,
Unto us a Son is given.
And the government will be upon His shoulder.
And His name will be called Wonderful, Counselor,
Mighty God, Everlasting Father, Prince of Peace.
Of the increase of His government and peace
There will be no end.
Upon the throne of David and over his kingdom,
To order it and establish it with judgment and justice
From that time forward, even forever.
The zeal of the Lord of hosts will perform this.

—ISAIAH 9:6–7

Jesus stood and cried out, saying, "If anyone thirsts, let him come to Me and drink. He who believes in Me, as the Scripture has said, out of his heart will flow rivers of living water."

—JOHN 7:37–38

By faith Sarah herself also received strength to conceive seed, and she bore a child when she was past the age, because she judged Him faithful who had promised.

—HEBREWS 11:11

Fruitful Days
98–100

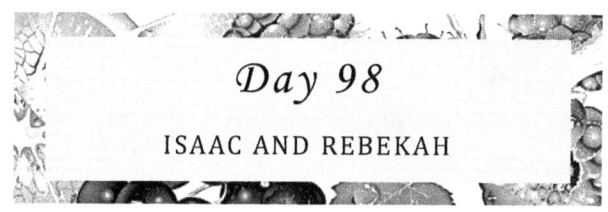

Day 98
ISAAC AND REBEKAH

We have focused on Abraham's life before he became a father, but we cannot end without discussing Isaac, who was the means through which the promise of descendants was fulfilled. Moreover Isaac, like Melchizedek, is one of the Torah's early messianic shadows. He most clearly typifies Christ on Mount Moriah, when both Isaac and the ram that becomes his substitute foreshadow Jesus, the Lamb of God slain in our stead.

After the binding of Isaac, Abraham receives the most glorious blessing yet. The Lord declares:

> Blessing I will bless you . . .; and your descendants will possess the gate of their enemies. In your seed all the nations of the earth shall be blessed, because you have obeyed My voice. (Gen. 22:16–18)

When Isaac's future wife Rebekah is leaving her father's house to get married, her family speaks a blessing over her that uncannily echoes God's blessing: "May your descendants possess The gates of those who hate them" (Gen. 24:60). This blessing is especially true of Rebekah's spiritual descendants, the church. As Jesus promised after Peter's confession, "On this rock I will build My church, *and the gates of Hades shall not prevail against it*" (Matt. 16:18). By rock Jesus means the revelation of who He is, and it must be the confession not only of Peter but of all who belong to the church or *ekklesia*: "You are the Christ, the Son of the living God" (v. 16).

When Rebekah is childless twenty years after marriage, Isaac "pleaded with the LORD" on her behalf (Gen. 25:21). In this too he foreshadows the great Intercessor, who prayed for us during His earthly ministry (Luke 22:32; John 17) and who is still interceding for us in heaven (Rom. 8:34; Heb. 7:25).

All three of the patriarchs had barren wives. But while Sarah's barrenness ended "because she judged Him faithful who had promised" (Heb. 11:11), and Rachel's because God "remembered" and "listened to her" (Gen. 30:22), *Rebekah's barrenness ended because her husband interceded for her*. Since Isaac is a type of Christ, the Bridegroom of the church, the ending of Rebekah's barrenness—and not with one child but with *two*—suggests that we become fruitful primarily because Jesus is interceding for us.

Fruitfulness is not merely about ending barrenness. It is also about stewarding the blessed life well. And the blessed life is not without its trials, as Rebekah's complicated pregnancy proves. It's no fun to have two boys jostling in your womb, but instead of fretting or complaining or doubting God or snapping at people, this godly woman chooses to *inquire of the Lord*.

Rebekah's question, "If all is well, why am I like this?" (Gen. 25:22), shows that she took her trial as an occasion to seek God. And the fact that God answers her is a reminder that if we are willing to seek the Lord, He is willing to speak to us.

READ: 1 John 3
REFLECT: Romans 8:34
PRAY: Ask the Lord which area you need to steward better and how you should steward it better today.

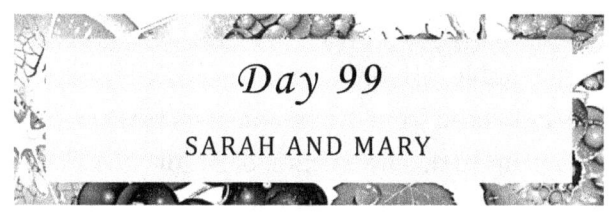

Day 99

SARAH AND MARY

Just as Isaac was promised to Abraham long before he was born, so also was the Messiah promised centuries before *He* was born. And both births were miracles. Humanly speaking, neither a virgin nor a barren ninety year old can bear a child. These were undeniable facts, yet each woman went from facts to faith and so obtained what had been promised.

Sarah received the strength to conceive the seed "because she judged Him faithful who had promised" (Heb. 11:11). Thus, even though she was barren and past childbearing, she conceived because she had the right view of God—that He is faithful to His promises.

Previously Sarah had lived by the facts. When she devised the disastrous plan to involve Hagar, she told Abraham, "The LORD has restrained me from bearing children" (Gen. 16:2). This was factually correct. God had indeed restrained her, but not because He did not want to grant what He Himself had promised. *God had restrained Sarah because Isaac's birth had to be a miracle, so Abraham and Sarah would be credited with their faith and nothing but their faith.*

Sarah's statement about being restrained by God contains a note of bitterness, and being restrained or confined always has the potential to embitter us towards God. In such situations we must diligently guard our heart, "lest any root of bitterness springing up cause trouble" (Heb. 12:15).

Sarah is delivered from the prison of facts when the Lord visits Abraham prior to the destruction of Sodom and Gomorrah and promises that Sarah will have a son in a year. Eavesdropping Sarah laughs in disbelief, and the Lord rebukes her, saying, "Is anything too hard for the LORD?" (Gen. 18:14). The rebuke transforms Sarah's view of God so that at last she sees Him as faithful, and this moves her from unbelief to the kind of faith it takes to produce an Isaac.

The essence of biblical faith is that it responds to God's question to Sarah with an emphatic *No!* It declares that *nothing* is too hard for the Lord. Or, to put it in Jesus' words, biblical faith says, "*With God all things are possible*" (Matt. 19:26).

Like Sarah, Mary the mother of Jesus also considered the facts. When the angel Gabriel announced the birth to her, she asked, "How can this be since I am a virgin?" (Luke 1:34). This was a legitimate question, so Gabriel answered it. But since she was already a woman of faith, Mary quickly moved past pondering the facts to making one of the most profound statements anyone has made in Scripture: "Behold the handmaid of the Lord; be it unto me according to your word" (v. 38 KJV).

Mary's words reflect total surrender to God's will. By calling herself a handmaid, she is saying that her will, like that of a bondslave, is not her own. She is willingly accepting whatever her Lord wants, no matter the cost. This is true surrender.

> READ: 1 John 4
> REFLECT: Matthew 19:26
> PRAY: Thank the Lord that nothing is too difficult for Him and commit a current problem to Him.

Day 100
THE WELLS OF SALVATION

Five times in Genesis 26 we are told that Isaac digs wells that yield water. This is not an inconsequential detail, for Isaac's wells have a special place in the redemption story. The wells prosper Isaac and his household even as the living water that Jesus has to offer brings life to many.

In His conversation with the woman at the well, Jesus said that if anyone drinks of the living water He gives, it will become within them "a fountain of water springing up into everlasting life" (John 4:14). Another time, on the last and greatest day of the Feast of Tabernacles in Jerusalem, Jesus had stood up in the Temple and cried out in a loud voice, "If anyone is thirsty, let him come to Me and drink. He who believes in Me, as the Scripture said, 'From his innermost being will flow rivers of living water'" (John 7:37–38 NASB). The next verse tells us that He was referring to the Holy Spirit.

When we commit our lives to Jesus, the Holy Spirit enters our "innermost being" and begins to flow in us and through us like a river. Just as a river changes and shapes the land through which it courses, as well as the debris drifting in its current, the Spirit transforms us both inwardly and outwardly. As we continually yield to Him, we manifest the fruit of the Spirit, proving that we are "neither barren nor unfruitful in the knowledge of our

Lord Jesus Christ" (2 Pet. 1:8). Outwardly, we become a blessing to others.

Scripture's final mention of the water of life echoes the invitation Jesus had issued at the Temple: "Let the one who is thirsty come; and let the one who wishes take the free gift of the water of life" (Rev. 22:17 NIV). These words tell us what is needed to avail of God's free gift of eternal life.

First, *we must be thirsty*. We must realize that we have a yearning within that nothing seems to be satisfying. This is our inbuilt thirst for God; and just as nothing but water can quench our physical thirst, nothing but God can quench our thirst for God. Next, *we must come and take*. Even a free gift has to be accepted.

We had noted on Day 2 that the Hebrew word for blessing, *berakah*, is similar to *berekah*, which is a reservoir where camels kneel as a resting-place. Just as a camel traversing the blistering expanse of a desert yearns for such an oasis, so every human heart craves the fountain of living waters. Or, to use the analogy that opens Psalm 42, *as the deer pants for streams of water*, so our soul thirsts for the living God.

Isaac's wells foreshadow this living water from the living God, and they point forward to the prophecy in Isaiah 12:1–3. When the word salvation is replaced with our Savior's Hebrew name, which means salvation, verse 3 reads: "Therefore with joy you will draw water From the wells of *Yeshua*."

> READ: *1 John 5*
> REFLECT: *John 7:37–38*
> PRAY: *Thank the Holy Spirit for all that He has done for you these 100 days and praise Him for what's ahead.*